RECOLLECTIONS & OTHER TRIVIA

Bob Mattox

authorHOUSE®

AuthorHouse™
1663 Liberty Drive, Suite 200
Bloomington, IN 47403
www.authorhouse.com
Phone: 1-800-839-8640

First published by AuthorHouse 12/10/2008

ISBN: 978-1-4389-1779-5 (sc)

Printed in the United States of America
Bloomington, Indiana

This book is printed on acid-free paper.

TABLE OF CONTENTS

Foreword	ix
Credits	xi
The Night the Airplane Landed	1
The Long Vote Count	3
Crockett and the Rain Machine	6
The Wrestling Match	9
The Fiddlers Festival	12
Crockett & The Bomb	16
When I Met the Prince	19
The Nucor Saga	21
The Jaycees	23
Eating Bear Meat	26
Didn't It Rain Children	29
Hotels, Tourist Courts, & Motels	32
Characters from the Past	35
Whose to Blame	38
The Renaissance	41
Houston County Development Foundation - Continued	44
Bird Hunting	48
More Hunting Stories	51
Bird Dogs & Snakes	53
A Memorable Trip	57
The Sound of Taps	60
Good Old Days?	63
God Bless America	66
Giving Advice	66
Acquiring Culture	69
Traffic on the Square	72
The Treasure Hunt	75

Movies of the Past   78
Packing for a Trip   81
Hindsight   84
Pigeons   87
Bits and Pieces   90
Back When   93
Mad Dogs   96
What's in a Name   100
Playing Football   102
What a Shame   105
Alarm Systems   107
Good Cooks & Others   110
The Swimming Pool   113
Eulogies   117
    Eulogy To Willie Hayne Knox   118
    Eulogy To Harold Mack (Red Bull) Walker   121
    Eulogy To Grady Lake   124
    Eulogy To Jim Dubcak   128
WWII & Seabiscuit   129
Diets Versus Common Sense   132
Egrets Have Come to Town   135
Snakes and Other Varmints   139
Buying a New Car   143
Staying in the Hospital   147
This Too Shall Pass   150
Don't Blame the System   154
On Being Sick   157
Social Security Or Insecurity?   160
Bar-B-Que Then & Now   164
Trinity River Authority – Fifty Years of Service   166
Time to Live-Time to Die   169
Stand on Whiskey   172

Yesterday and Possum Hunting   175
In the Army   178
The Real Thing   181
Looking for Help   184
A New Life   186
The Rain Crow   190
Change Ready Or Not - Like It Or Not   193
An Address to the Crockett Rotary Club   197
The Family Reunion   201
A Near Experience   204
Old Times Dere But Not Forgotten   207
One Man's Opinion   210
College Mascots   213
Old Customs   215
Getting with It   218
Winds of Fate   220

FOREWORD

Due to good genes and Medical Science I have lived a span of life from the horse and buggy days to men landing on the moon. During this time I have been sustained by a God given sense of humor that enabled me to enjoy the good times and to hide the tears in times of sadness.

I have been a witness to and participant in all the stories contained in this book that with certain embellishment are all true.

Rather than take all these memories to the grave with me I have been urged by family and friends to write them down.

I leave it to you readers to judge whether the effort has been worth while.

Bob Mattox
Crockett, Texas
December, 2007

CREDITS

To: Dorothy Harrison, who without her encouragement, dedication, and hard work, this project would have never gotten off the ground.

To: Carol Watson whose experience paved the way for this endeavor.

And last to my understanding wife of sixty years, who spent long hours editing and correcting my inept attempt at writing.

The Night the
Airplane Landed

I saw in the news awhile back about an airplane that landed on a highway. I didn't see any big deal about this because it landed in broad daylight. I remember when one landed on a highway here in Crockett only it was at night.

It happened one night back in the late fifties when in the closing minutes of a football game in Bull Dog stadium a twin engine plane with no lights on kept circling the stadium cutting its engines on and off. This was a clear signal to the late Roy Garner, Doug Arnold, and other pilots of WWII that it was in trouble.

Just about then the game ended and a bunch of us jumped in our cars and headed for the old Madisonville highway. Back then this was the main highway to Madisonville before the loop was built.

The reason this strip of highway was picked for the landing was because there was no other place for a large plane to land. At that time there was a grass strip behind K.I.V.Y. radio station, but suitable only for small planes and dare devil pilots to land on.

We lined up on each side of the highway about fifty yards apart with the cars pointing West with the lights on.

The plane came in over the Dr. Dean house and made a smooth landing.

Two men got out of the plane and explained that they had taken delivery of the plane in Ft. Worth and were headed for College Station when an electrical malfunction knocked out all the instruments and lights on the plane.

They decided to fly from town to town reading the name on the water towers. When they got to Crockett, and without a compass they didn't know which direction College Station was and being low on gas decided to land.

When they discovered that they were less than an hour from College Station and all they had to do was to follow Highway 21, to our utter amazement they decided to take off.

They taxied back up to the Dean house while we turned our lights back on, gunned the motors and took off as smoothly as they landed. With our mouths still open we watched them disappear into the night. Since we never heard or read of a plane crash on Highway 21 we figured that they made it.

THE LONG VOTE COUNT

We are reading and hearing a lot bout politics lately probably more than we want to. Politics is an art. To master the art you have to learn to tell the truth five or six different ways before you tell a lie. I tried it once.

I let the Crockett Power Structure, at that time, flatter me into running for the Crockett School Board. They assured me that with their money and influence I wouldn't have to do a thing there was no way my opponent could beat me. I didn't do anything. but he did beat me so bad that I didn't go to town for a week.

As the old song goes, time takes care of everything, and years later I let Dan Julian who was the County Democratic Chairman, talk me into being the Election Judge for Crockett Precinct Three. Now Precinct three then, was worse than Duval County in that it was made up mostly of minorities who were hauled to the polls where someone cast their ballot for them.

After belatedly checking around, I realized what I had stepped into. The first thing I did was to appoint Mr. Van Doyle, a respected black man of the Community, as an Election Judge. He was the first Black ever to serve in that post. I lined up what I thought were plenty of ballot counters to do the job. This was not only a presidential election but included a hot Sheriff's race which always got the voters out.

The morning dawned eternal bright and clear and the voters started showing up in droves. If that wasn't enough, here came a slew of Republican Poll Watchers, duty bound to see that we held an honest election. That's about the first time that the Republicans in Houston County came out of the closet to save the world from the Democrats.

To restore some order I swore them in as Election Judges and put them to work. I had no more trouble with them. About this time here came the first car load of voters and the person who was to vote for them. I stopped the haulers at the door and swore them in as election judges. That also took care of that problem. As the voters kept pouring in, I realized we were facing a record voter's turn out, and that the lovely vote counters who had spent the morning visiting, doing their nails, and sharing a leisurely lunch were way behind. Adding to that was a shortage of supplies and other things new to we green personnel.

To show what kind of day it was about the time our polls closed, here came a Marcell Ledbetter type pulp wood cutter who said he came to vote for Mr. Elmer. He was some what taken aback when we told him Mr. Elmer was running for Mayor of Lovelady and the polls would be closed by the time he got there. He jumped in his truck and took off. I wondered what he told Mr. Elmer.

The polls finally closed and my beautiful ballot counters were furiously trying to keep up the tally. We brought in food to eat as they worked. As the night wore on I would stick my head in to check on them. As the long count went on I noticed that their lipstick was not as straight as usual, their hair was somewhat disarrange, and other signs of a breakdown in civilized behavior.

About seven Sunday morning, I learned that they had finished counting. When I went in to get the ballot boxes I hardly recognized any of them. To say the least it wasn't a pretty sight that greeted me.

To further add insult to injury some of the poll watchers reported me to the State Election Bureau charging that I helped voters cast their ballots. When a reporter called me, I told him that the poll watchers just didn't want the black people to vote. That was the magic word then as would be now and that was the end of that.

On the way to the Sheriffs office with the ballot boxes that bright Sunday morning, I realized that I had held two election at one time; My First and Last.

By the way, Lyndon Johnson won.

CROCKETT AND THE
RAIN MACHINE

Since the dawn of time man has been trying to control the weather mostly by trying to make it rain and in some rare instances, trying to make it stop, without much success at either.

Most of the efforts to bring rain have been of a spiritual nature with prayer being the main effort. Added to that has been dancing, beating of drums, fasting, self torture, and many more appeals being made to their God of Rain. Some have resorted to a self proclaimed rain maker who guarantees results.

I had an old timer tell me with a straight face about the Deacons of a rural church, desperate for rain, hired a noted rain maker to try and bring rain. His fee based on the amount of rain he caused.

He went to work, praying and shouting in soul lifting fashion, in tongues never heard before by these simple people. Finally it began to rain in a gentle shower, then harder and harder, coming down in buckets and barrels, washing out crops, roads, and even trees.

The rain maker had long stopped praying when it finally stopped. When he presented his bill at the Deacons meeting one of the Deacons voted not to pay him. When asked why, he replied that the man orta know better than to pray for rain when the wind was out of the East like that.

Speaking of praying for rain I am reminded of a prayer for rain offered by Judge Robert M. Williamson, a legendary man in early Texas history widely known for his gift as a stump speaker. On one occasion he was invited by a revival preacher to offer a prayer for rain. The crowd was composed largely of farmers who had been suffering the effects of a drought. The Judge welcomed the opportunity and used this prayer.

"Oh Lord, thou divine Father, the supreme ruler of the universe, who holdest the thunder and lightening in thy hands, and from the clouds givest rain to make crops for thy children, look down with pity upon thy children who now face ruin for lack of rain upon their crops. Oh Lord send us down a down pour that will cause the crops to fruit in all their glory and the earth to turn again to that beauteous green that comes from abundant showers.

Lord send us a bounteous one that will make corn ears shake hands across the row and not one of those rizzly-drizzly rains that will only make nubbins that all hell can't shuck."

We don't know if the Judge's prayer produced the needed rain but if there was ever a prayer that should have moved the Lord this was it.

Back to the subject at hand, Crockett's rain making machine. In the mid nineteen fifties, Houston County along with the rest of the Southwest was suffering from a prolonged drought and it had gotten real serious with water rationing and livestock suffering.

There was a man in Colorado, named Dr. Irving Krick who came up with the idea that if he could get silver oxide crystals up into moisture bearing clouds it would produce rain. One method was to drop them from and airplane, the other to send them up from the ground. That's where Crockett came into the picture.

The ground method used was a generator that heated the crystals and sent them up into the air. Such a machine was located at my old Humble service station across from the Methodist Church.

Now we didn't just turn the machine on when we wanted to we had to wait for a phone call. It was supposed to work like this, for example if rain clouds of the right kind appeared over Lovelady and the wind was from the South at Five miles per hour, then the clouds should be over Crockett in about three hours and that's when we turned on the machine.

I do not remember our action ever causing any rain over Crockett at the time, but it did rain later on when the drought ended as has happened since the dawn of time.

THE WRESTLING MATCH

I see that some organization is going to bring a Semi-Pro wrestling event to Crockett. This takes me back over fifty years to another similar event held here in Crockett. This event was promoted by the Crockett Jaycees who would do anything to make a dollar.

This was in 1957 when there were very few televisions sets and those being very primitive by today's standards and being offered in only black and white and requiring a massive antenna on the roof with a motor to make the thing change direction.

Back then reception was limited to a few stations and very poor reception at that. Nothing from the north, only Shreveport to the east, Bryan to the west, to the south sometime Houston, but of all things Galveston came in clearer than any other station. That is where they had wrestling and more wrestling and that's what most people watched. They were either more naive then or it beat nothing, so wrestling it was.

That is when the Crockett Jaycees got the bright idea of bringing wrestling to Crockett. I presume it was a sanctioned event of the Wrestling Federation, because we had to have a standard rig set up, referee, and a time keeper. Someone sent in an application for a Time Keepers License in my name and I was issued License number

792 by the Texas Boxing and Wrestling Law, under Supervision of Commissioner of Labor. It cost $2.50.

The event was held in the old Crockett High School gym where the wrestlers brought the ring set up and the referee with them. My time keeper's station was right against one corner of the ring. I had a card table, a metal folding chair, a stop watch, and a bell. I really felt important.

The wrestlers were a pretty nice looking bunch and you could tell they were on friendly terms with each other. We thought they were pretty big, but of course nothing compared to the three and four hundred pound eating machines we see today. They were big enough that we didn't comment on their hair.

As I remember we had a pretty big crowd, mostly dyed in the wool wrestling fans. The wrestlers had themselves divided into the good guys and the bad guys. They really put on a good show and had the crowd with them.

One of the acts called for the bad guy to throw the good guy out of the ring. Now that was a real crowd pleaser to everyone but me, because the tossed wrestler landed on my time keepers table crushing it and my chair, and I thought at the time had broken my legs and back. They picked me up dusted me off and the matches went on.

To excite the crowd they would manage to scratch each other to bring a little blood. The crowd was really into it and cried for more blood. It was about to get out of hand.

Just about then an old man from the north end of the County got completely carried away and jumped into the ring and in the vernacular of East Texas "stobbed" one of the bad guys in the thigh. Since he used the small blade of his knife it didn't do much damage. That's when the boys with the pretty hair discovered that wrestling, especially in Crockett, could be dangerous and it broke up the wrestling match.

The Jaycees stated that they were glad that there were no serious injuries, over looking the fact that I could hardly walk for a week.

If any organization decides to promote an event that requires a time keeper, sorry I cannot help you, my license has expired.

THE FIDDLERS FESTIVAL

It is hard to believe that another year has passed and it is Fiddler's Festival time again. This will be either the 65th or 66th anniversary of the event depending on the Chamber of Commerce date of 1937 or the date we have always recognized as being 1936. At any rate it has been going on a long time.

It was started by Barker Tunstall, an old time fiddler and piano tuner, who got together a bunch of old fiddler friends to come to Crockett and perform. The square was blocked off and the fiddlers played on the Court House lawn. It ended with a dance on the square. This went on until after the WWII, when the boys came home from the War and organized the Junior Chamber of Commerce.

At the urging of the down town merchants and to expand its activities, it was moved to the park. It was held in the old Livestock Pavilion which had a stage and could accommodate a large crowd. It really took off when the late Roy Garner got a hold of it, changed its format, and got the idea to name it "The World Championship Fiddler's Contest." The name was patented and according to Roy, it prevented Athens, Texas from using the title.

Roy Garner was a great fan of fiddle music becoming acquainted with it through his maternal grandfather, Uncle Tooz Lively and even giving it a try in his younger days. He was the first emcee when it moved to the park and continued for some twenty years afterward. With his natural line of bull, he was good at it.

The format back then was similar to the one used today with the older fiddlers starting off the morning program playing old tunes such as Black Mountain Rag, Boil Them Cabbages Down, Gray Eagle, Sally Johnson, Bitter Creek, Old Joe Clark, Eighth of January, Bake Them Hoe Cakes Brown, Cotton Eyed Joe, The Orange Blossom Special, and other old tunes learned by ear and passed down from generation to generation. They all sounded pretty much the same to us but they knew the difference. The younger players would play during the day.

Different bands and entertainers would perform during the day. Some of these were really good, having been booked early by Jim Gibbs and Bill Carter who saw their potential early on.

The climax of the event was the dance held that night in the Old Exhibit building. Usually several bands, some free of charge, would play for the event. Many last minute things had to be done such as borrowing all the shop fans in town, putting tubs of ice in front of the fans, putting corn meal on the floor, getting a P.A. system, setting up proper lights, and so forth.

Always saved for last was the crisis of getting a piano for the dance. Now the only one available with the means to transport it was owned by a man who didn't believe in drinking and dancing. Every year we had to send a delegation of Jaycees, who were experienced in stretching the truth, to promise him that we would do our best to prevent anyone from drinking or dancing. The Texas Rangers could not have done this and he knew this as well as we did but at least it salved his conscience, and ours didn't need salving. This was a game we played each year.

The Festival and Crockett got national news in 1968 when Jefferson Davis, publisher of the Crockett Democrat, at a news convention in Galveston presented President Richard Nixon with two coon skin caps for his daughters.

The zenith of the Fiddler's Festival was reached later that year when Crockett was invited to send a delegation of fiddlers to the Hemisfair in San Antonio. The town quickly raised the money to do this.

Roy quickly rounded up a group of fiddlers that had performed here including Jesse Johnson, Leon Selp, Louis Franklin, J.T. McBride, fourteen year old Gordon Towsend, Mary Sampler, the only woman up to that time to win a championship, and many others. He rounded up several western bands also.

Included in the group were six lovely members of the Beta Sigma Phi dressed in buck skin skirts and coon skin hats. They made a big hit as they passed out brochures and answered question about Crockett and Houston County. As President of the Houston County Development Foundation, that sponsored the trip, Peggy and I went along.

The first performance was Thursday noon in front of some fifteen hundred people, mostly news reporters, another that night, before another large crowd. The Hemisfair didn't open to the general public until Saturday so Friday we had the whole run of the place.

Friday was something special with a reception by Governor John Connally and his lovely wife Nellie and including many well known people. Roy and his group put on a show that drew praise from the Governor and others.

Two more outstanding shows were done on Saturday with a final show on Sunday that was recorded and is now in the archives of the Institute of Texan Culture in San Antonio. Later, the group had an invitation by an official of the Grand Old Opera to appear on their show, but didn't have the incentive to attempt something like this again.

This was once in a life time event that could probably have never happened before and in all probability will never happen again. I feel most fortunate to have been a witness to this event.

CROCKETT & THE BOMB

Since September 11th it seems that this Country is finally waking up to the dangers we face not only man made but from nature itself. We have a color coded plan, a 911 telephone system alert plan, deep under ground shelters for Congress and government officials, and even on the local level we have a plan to get our County officials and employees safely away from the square in case of a bomb scare. I guess the people who work around the square have enough sense to take off when the Court House empties. We know we have had other disasters not caused by terrorist but by the fault of some one. The New London school explosion in 1937 that killed almost three hundred school children was caused by a natural gas leak that went undetected because it had no odor; the fertilizer ship that blew up at Texas City in 1947 leaving over thirty five hundred dead and injured when the cargo was accidentally set afire. Then we have the so called acts of God like the 1900 hurricane in Galveston that cost over ten thousand lives killed or missing. In our own life time hurricane Carla emptied the Gulf coast and sent refugees North, filling every spare bed in Houston County. Some things we just can not prepare for and I am afraid that is the case today with our so called Warning Systems. We tried that once and it was an expensive government boon doggle then and I am afraid it will turn out that way today.

To get back to the subject of Crockett and the bomb we go back to the earlier sixties during the Cuban Missile Crisis when the threat of an A-Bomb being lunched from Cuba to one of our large cities was pretty real. A National Civil Defense Program was launched from Washington and Crockett, not wanting to be left behind, under the direction of the Reverend Hunter Morris, started its own program. Now you must understand that nobody expected a bomb to be dropped on Crockett, Lovelady, Grapeland, Porter Springs, or Hopewell, or other centers of population but it was the fall out from a bomb that would get you maybe slowly but it would get you. Since Houston and Dallas would be primary targets we had to worry about the wind bringing the so called "Fall Out" to us. Of course we had to have a warning signal. This was done with two towers, one behind City Hall, and one behind the Episcopal Church, which when activated produced a wootle wootle sound which was much easier on the ears that the diabolical sounds emanating from Hades that our fire and emergency vehicles emit. Since I don't remember seeing one come by my house without the lights flashing and the horrible sounds going makes me believe that these things come on when they turn the key on. The other night when the car knocked out the lights I heard a new sound when a fire truck passed and made a barfing sound like a Brahma bull would make with a range cube stuck in his throat. I don't want to be little the job our emergency personnel do but I sometimes wish it could be done a little quieter.

The instructions from Washington to the Rev. Morris was to draw up a plan for the City and County Officials that when the wootle, wootle sounded they were to take shelter in the available basements in town which was supposed to be stocked with food and water to last five days. The fact that few of these basements had restroom facilities was lost on the Civil Defense officials in Washington. Just before this plan got started the Rev. Morris moved to Austin and I was appointed Civil Defense Director for Crockett and it fell my lot to decide who would get refuge in the limited shelters available. Also how to get the food, water and other amenities into the shelters and above all advise the chosen officials what to tell their families to do when they went under ground. I might add that several families built their own bomb shelters which are still standing but they tried to keep it quite because they were afraid some might fill it up before they could get in themselves. I decided that I didn't want any part of assigning people to shelters so my instructions to the people were if the fall out comes from the South head North as fast as you can and keep going till you run out of danger and if it comes from the North you figure it out. In retrospect I guess we had a pretty good plan because we did not lose anyone from Houston County to Atomic Fall Out.

WHEN I MET THE PRINCE

I notice in the paper that President Bush has invited Crown Prince Abdullah of Saudi Arabia to visit his ranch in Texas. I met Crown Prince Saud, later to become King of Saudi Arabia, once. It happened this way. In 1946, at the tender age of 26, I was a freshman at Texas A&M., thinking I wanted to become a Horse Doctor until I found out that I had to pass chemistry. Now the country high school that I graduated from not only did not teach chemistry but never heard of it. I learned about hogs, cattle, chickens, fruit trees and other worth while stuff but nothing about chemistry. After failing chemistry once, and repeating it, I learn that sodium chloride was table salt and that impressed my parents. I changed majors. Since I wanted to become a horse doctor I got a job at the horse barn feeding, watering, and exercising the stallions we had there. The pro shop and golf course is where we used to have the horse barn.

To get back to my story when the Prince visited the A&M campus we were ordered to display all the animals in front of the horse barn. We brought out a famous racing stallion, a five gaited stallion, a beautiful golden palomino, a King Ranch quarter stud, a Shetland stallion, used for display purposes only since he had been kicked in his private parts by a mare and would not get within fifty feet of one, and we even brought old Pat Murphy the celebrated off spring of a mare mule and a Morgan Stallion, who was twenty-six years old and blind but he would strike a pose.

When the big black limo passed by we saw the Prince leaning out the window looking at the horses. We put the horses up and went to lunch and this being Saturday every one but us peons took off for the weekend. Soon after I got a call saying that the Prince was at the Dairy barn and wanted to see a Texas cowboy and a quarter horse. I sure was not a cowboy but being the only one available I put on my one pair of boots, and old work shirt, and my old work hat, went down to the barn, saddled Kinganuda, the famous King Ranch quarter horse, and headed for the dairy barns about two miles away.

When I rode up the Prince came over and started looking at the horse. Right behind him came three or four of the roughest characters you ever saw. They were dressed in those white sheets that they wear, with knives big enough to cut sugar cane with, hanging at their sides and each with a Tommy gun hidden under the sheets. The Prince didn't offer to shake hands and I sure wasn't going to stick my hand out and maybe get it cut off so when he turned away I turned the horse around and rode into the sun set. With the connections that I had with the rulers of Saudi Arabia I thought down through the years that I might be called on by our State Department to go over there and help solve some problems but I guess they have been pretty busy.

The Nucor Saga

I read where the Vulcraft employees were recognized for their outstanding work record. I also read in the U.S. News & World Report a very complimentary article about their parent corporation, Nucor. They are an outstanding company and a tremendous asset to our County. I thought it might be well to tell the story of how they got here. I had a man tell me awhile back that if Crockett had cooperated with the company that the plant would have been located in Crockett instead of Grapeland. That is not the case at all.

One night in the early sixties Dewey Lloyd, a neighbor of mine, called and said that a cousin of his wife, Charlene, had dropped in for a visit. He was from Indiana and was sent to East Texas to look for a possible location for a steel mill. I immediately got in touch with the Movers and Shakers of Houston County, back when we had such people, and they went to work. In no time they had the President and several executives down here, feeding them fish & hush puppies, corn on the cob, and other East Texas goodies, washed down with appropriate beverage, and showing them possible sites for a plant. I might add that this plant made steel. It required lots of iron ore gravel. They left with a good impression of Houston County.

In later contacts with them we learned that a company named Nuclear Corporation of America had bought their company. The named was later changed to Nucor. The whole process started over with Nucor with the Executives being brought to Houston County and shown several locations. One location being where Ampacet is now located. This ninety acres of land with rail road siding available was bought by the people of Houston County and made available to Nucor. The great day came when the Executives of Nucor came to pick a site for their Vulcraft plant. We were showing them the land we had for the plant when they were shown the Grapeland location which they chose for the plant. There was no doubt that it was a better site than the land we had bought. We were glad that it would be in Houston County and would employ local people.

Before we started the celebration we learned from George Bartee, the Mayor of Grapeland, that the City didn't have the ten thousand dollars to run utilities to the site. The Houston County Development Foundation leaders, which I will tell about in a later article, came to Grapeland and told them to raise what money they could and the other Communities would raise the rest that was needed. This was done. That shows what kind of leaders we had at one time in this County and sadly lack today. That leadership produced many great things for our County which we will talk about later.

And now to paraphrase a smooth talking radio commentator, "NOW YOU KNOW THE REST OF THE STORY."

The Jaycees

The Crockett Junior Chamber of Commerce, better known as the Jaycees, made its appearance in Crockett in 1947 and was eagerly received by the home coming Veterans of World War II who had left Crockett as boys and came back as men.

These men had been out in another world and done things that they never dreamed of ever doing. Many had risked their lives, some had been wounded. They had seen the elephant and were ready to get home and get on with living. Most were not satisfied with what they found when they returned home. Nothing had changed and they were expecting change.

Some adjusted, either by finding jobs, going into business, or continuing their education. Some could not make the adjustment finding life too dull after spending time in exciting places and around a different kind of people who accepted them in some cases because of the uniform that they wore. Some were not satisfied with the high school sweethearts or in some cases the young brides that they had left behind. They just plain could not adjust.

Some brought back brides from different parts of the Country and some from foreign Countries. Young women who didn't know our customs and were expected to learn our dialect, endure our heat, eat peas once or twice a day, peas that they fed their cattle back home. Some couldn't make the change and left.

For those who choose to stay here the Jaycees was a perfect outlet for their energies and so organized a chapter in 1947 with H.B. (Mutt) Knox the first President. The Jaycees took off from there. They moved the fiddle contest to the Park and made it nationally known. They had a concession stand built on skids and took it to every function where they could serve food and make some money. The old stand that stood by the old pavilion was recently torn down and replaced.

In addition they took and active part in every worth while project under taken in the County including the Houston County Lake, the Hospital, the Library, the first Nursing Home, and the first modern motel, a modern telephone system for the County, the Airport, the Loop, and their crowning glory was the swimming pool. This story deserves an article all it own and will be covered in detail later on.

The age limit for active membership in the Jaycees was thirty-five. After then you became an Exhausted Rooster. Most went on working after that moving into the Houston County Development Foundation which is a story within its self.

When you call the honor roll of the surviving members who are still, in their own way, trying to make this town a better place to live in, you include the names of H.B. (Mutt) Knox, Jake Caprielian, Dr. John McCall, Dan Julian, Jim Gibbs, Grady Lake, Vaughn Reynen, Dr. Carl

Murray, W.H. Holcomb, and myself. If I have missed anyone you can blame it on advanced age.

The term Exhausted Rooster made us feel some what old at the time but would be a compliment now for most of us to be called exhausted instead of just flat wore out as most of us are now. However we have one consolation and that is the memories that we did something that in all probability will never be done again.

EATING BEAR MEAT

Visited the Bob Bullock Texas History Museum in Austin last week and was really impressed. It's probably the nearest thing to getting your money's worth this day and time. For less than $25.00 per adult you can park, take in the shows, and get lunch. Children about half that.

I was somewhat surprised at how much space was devoted to Davy Crockett and his exploits. They had his famous quote to the folks in Tennessee "that they could all go to hell that he was going to Texas" and his freely offered advice "to be sure you are right and go ahead." They didn't have a quote from his wife and family that he hauled off and left in Tennessee. I would like to have heard that.

I was surprised that Crockett just got mentioned briefly as a place where he camped three days on his was to the Alamo but what really got my attention was that he claimed to have killed 103 bears in one year. That's about two a week. Black bears can weigh up to 500 pounds and that's a lot of meat to get rid of. It's pretty hard to get rid of the meat from two bears as I found out one time.

Pearl Harbor was attacked on December 7, 1941 and by Xmas our outfit was scattered from Ft. Lewis, Washington, to Portland Oregon, to Northern California, guarding bridges, tunnels, ship loading docks, and lots of time just looking out for anything the Japanese might harm. Incidentally they could have easily done this because we had very little to stop them, with our World War I weapons in the hands of green troops.

It was a wide eyed group of country boys, fresh from the Great Depression, that jumped out up there. Boys who had never been very far from home, who had never eaten fancy foods, like a shrimp cocktail, or a broiled steak, or had a mixed drink, boys from deep East Texas whose folks had always cooked inside and gone to the toilet outside. Everything completely different.

It was not all bad for the rough lumberjacks, long shore men, and others really took to us. You could not pay for anything when they were around. Part of this could have been patriotism but we finally figured out it was mostly to hear us talk. They had never been around country boys from Texas that talked like we did and naturally we laid it on pretty thick. But back to my story.

We were stationed in an old C.C.C. camp about halfway between the Oregon border and San Francisco when we became acquainted with a State Bear Hunter. It was against the law to kill a bear in California but if a bear killed some of your livestock, mostly sheep, the State would send the bear hunter to get the bear.

He was a big fellow, wore a big black hat, and talked in a slow deep voice. He took a liking to us and invited us out to his house which was located in a big canyon. I will always remember eating fresh cherries from a big tree in the yard and seeing a pack of the biggest, roughest chewed up bear hounds you ever saw. We foolishly told him that we would like to try some bear meat and he said the first time he got one close to camp he would call us.

We got his call one morning telling us that he had one close to camp. Several of us got a truck and took off. The ranch was way up in the mountains and I thought we would never get there.

He had killed one bear and when he went to the ranch house to call us one dog followed him and treed a bear on the way back. He killed that one too. The scene that greeted us was two huge black bears on the ground with dogs feeding on sheep meat. That should have been enough warning to us but no we cut off four quarters and lugged them back to the trucks and on to camp.

Another minus on my part of this affair was that I helped skin out the quarters and you can believe what you read, when they say a skinned out bear paw looks just like a human hand.

With memory of feeding dogs, the bear paw, the dark red color and sweet taste of the meat, and the job the army cooks did on cooking it, I lost my taste for bear meat and have not regained it to this day.

Didn't It Rain Children

Mother Nature can be a benign, kind, and caring force in our life bringing us the warm sun, the gentle rain, and seasons of abundant harvest that sustain us. On the other side of the coin it can be a terrible adversary bringing drought, fires, hurricanes, tornadoes, and too much rain at one time as we have witnessed lately.

The three feet of water that fell on the Hill Country last week was just a drop in the bucket compared to the great Biblical Flood but it wreaked havoc with the hundreds of people who court disaster by building their homes in the one hundred year flood plain.

The hundred year flood is an area designated by the U. S. Corps of Engineers as an area that can expect at least one flood in one hundred years. Now it doesn't say that there can't be more than one which has been proven throughout history. We here in Houston County find it difficult to identify with this situation because we are fortunate in two ways. First, we found the high ground and our fore fathers had the good judgment to build on it.

It doesn't seem like twelve years since we had a major flood here in the Trinity River water shed but we sure had one back in 1990 when it rained all over the State causing massive flooding. It even flooded in Marfa, Texas where local legend has it that the town only got two inches during the Biblical Flood.

As mentioned, it rained so much it filled up all the lakes in the northern part of the State causing them to open the flood gates on their lakes releasing a wall of water that flooded the Trinity River bottom lands. When the river came out on 7-J land near Midway, it covered miles on Highway 21 with more than four feet of water,

All this water poured into Lake Livingston causing them to open their flood gates thereby releasing over 103,000 cubic feet per second to race down country. As I reported a few years ago this is when Bush One visited the lake spillway and his limo got stuck.

No sooner had this flood hit Liberty, Dayton, and other low lying Counties than howl went up from all those people who had repeatedly built down next to the river and had been flooded out. Many had been paid several times by a benevolent Government, (with your money), and told not to rebuild down there. Many made a good living out of this practice.

The local politicians made political hay out of this blaming everyone they could think of, for their citizens getting flooded out when in many cases they were the ones who sold them the property in the first place. Makes you wonder about people.

A young television reporter who interviewed some of the squatters who lived on the river banks and listened to their tales of woe wondered aloud after she went off the air if any of the residents had any teeth. It was pretty obvious that they didn't and obvious that they were short on brains also.

We are hearing the same cry from the affluent Hill Country citizens who want the government to replace their beautiful homes down on the river banks figuring that they will be long gone when the next hundred year flood hits. Get your pocket book ready.

Hotels, Tourist Courts, & Motels

We have come a long way from the old three story Crockett Hotel, to the crude tourist court cabins out by four mile park on Hwy 19, to the Twin Oaks Courts on N. 4th St. to the San Man Motel on S. 4th St., to the Kings Inn Motel on the East Loop, to the Crockett Inn on the Loop, to the Embers Motel on the Loop, and now a Holiday Inn on the Loop.

Before World War II, the Crockett Hotel was just about it when it came to a place to spend the night in Crockett the crude cabins by four mile park being mostly a place to buy bootleg whiskey. Then the Twin Oaks Courts, and then the San Man Motel came into being and these plus the Crockett Hotel provided a good clean place to spend the night but without the amenities that we take for granted today. The travelers wanted more and that created a demand for a modern motel.

This demand was met by an executive of Hughes Tool Company named Fred Ayers who saw a need for a modern facility here in Crockett and he built one. It was named the Kings Inn. It was located next to E.T.M.C. where the Professional Building is located. It was first class with dinning facilities, a swimming pool, and the most popular spot in the whole motel, a watering hole, where the "Power Structure" gathered each afternoon after work for an attitude adjustment session.

It had a most unique arrangement to serve liquor. Under the law at that time you could not buy a drink but as a member you could put your own bottle with your name on it under the bar and drink out of your bottle. Of course that soon got completely out of control because if somebody's bottle was empty he simply got one out of someone else's bottle. I don't remember what provision was made for a guest who wanted a drink and didn't have a bottle. Maybe that's what happened to the missing booze from the members supply.

It was a fun place to go. You could learn what was going on in town, hear the latest stories and jokes, and usually get in on some prank being played on someone. I remember one afternoon when a prominent business man who was on the corpulent side and whose main claim to exercise was opening pasture gates, when he didn't have a passenger to do it, boasted that he could walk around the loop. The crowd bet him $50.00 that he couldn't. While he was getting ready one of the local funeral home owners called and had a hearse (no ambulances then) come out to follow him. We all lined up behind the hearse and followed him around the loop. He won the $50.00. We thought that was great fun. If you tried it today you would probably be killed or at least arrested.

Crockett has always been, and still is, one of the wettest dry towns in Texas. Every local option election to vote the town wet has been soundly defeated. It was always amusing to see some the very people who so piously denounced the sale of liquor in Crockett be among the first at the bar in the afternoon.

The old Kings Inn changed hands a couple of times and finally because of competition and the escalating value of the property it stood on finally closed its doors. It set the pattern for the modern motels to follow.

The new Holiday Inn is touted to offer many advantages to Crockett one that has not been mentioned is that we can spend the night there and get smart. Maybe not as smart as the group that stayed at a Holiday Inn Express that we see so much of on television lately, however; I don't think we would have to spend a full night there to get smarter than the idiot who sticks his tongue out and wiggles it up and down.

CHARACTERS FROM THE PAST

Crockett like many small East Texas towns had their so called characters. People who stood out from some physical or mental characteristic or some unusual trait they possessed. We embrace them all with our love and memories.

There was Pat a small disabled man who probably suffered from Polio when he was young. Although he was small he carried a heavy leather valise, as they used to be called, crammed full of mysterious articles that we never saw. Some of the articles were for young men too timid to ask for them at the drug store. He probably didn't make much money off the timid young men. If Viagra had been available back then he could have made a lot of money off timid old men.

Columbus was another character that misfortune struck at an early age leaving him severely handicapped. He didn't complain or give up. He did about the only thing he was capable of doing and that was to parch peanuts and sell them from a kid's wagon that he pulled along. They were real good and he only charged a nickel a bag.

He was a likable fellow and never did anyone any harm. One day some of the local wags who used to hang around the Sanitary Barber Shop offered to pay for a dandruff treatment for Columbus. The medicine used belonged to a local doctor and it burned like liquid fire.

The barber applied it to Columbus' head. After about a minute the heat got so bad the barber began to rinse it off. Unfortunately Columbus had a nose that stuck almost straight up and the water was pouring into his nose and he couldn't get up. When he finally broke free a broken fire hose could not have spread more water than he did, most of it going on the wags who caused it all. We never found out if the treatment worked or not but Columbus never requested another one.

Then there was Louis, the gentle one, who had the mind of a child but the body of a giant. He stood over six feet tall and probably weighted close to three hundred pounds, and didn't know his own strength. His daily routine was to meet each train, deliver his papers, ride with Mr. Crowe on the Railway Express truck, get his daily donut, and go to the movies.

He had a game he played on his paper customers each day. He would try to slip up on them and slam the paper down. Everyone played the game with him and would play like they were frightened out of their wits. He would almost fall down laughing.

He had a special seat for his daily doughnut and woe to the stranger who happened to be sitting there. Same thing for anyone who occupied his extra wide seat at the Ritz theater. It is said that one day a stranger who didn't move quick enough was gently picked up by Louis and stood in the isle.

I had an incident that happened with Louis once that is fresh in my memory today. He was crossing the street one day when I playfully slipped up behind and grabbed him and yelled boo. He casually brushed my arm away and in the process almost dislocated my shoulder and just about ruined my watch which I found across the street in the gutter. I am some what a slow learner but I never tried that again.

He had a thing about the weather and always wanted it to rain. Some one had told him that Jim Gibbs out at K.I.V.Y. radio station could make it rain. No matter how many times he saw me each day he would invariable ask me to call Jim Gibbs and tell him to make it rain. As far as I know Jim could never pull this off.

These characters and others that followed are all gone. Just like the sunshine and the rain and a ripple on the water, here one minute and gone the next, leaving no trace of their passing.

Whose to Blame

I was always taught that if you did something wrong you accepted the blame and tried to make up for it. Try as I might, I cannot reconcile myself to accept the blame myself, that my generation have had placed on us. Things of the past that we absolutely had nothing to do with.

We didn't take the land from the Indians, take part in the 1923 race riot in Rosewood, Florida, cause the Holocaust, mistreat the Mexican guest worker, inter the Japanese during WWII, have anything to do with unfair loans to black farmers, or many of the other things we are being blamed for. We will probably be blamed for Eve eating the apple before this is over with.

We **ARE** to blame for letting things get out of hand resulting in the ridiculous and almost obscene situation we have created today, where unscrupulous lawyers and their greedy clients, many who simply want something for nothing, are suing everybody and everything under the sun for every dime that they can get their dirty hands on. We are to blame because we have not demanded that the court laws be changed to stop the worst of these abuses.

We wonder who are these naive and misguided people who are responsible for these huge awards. Where do they think the money will come from? Common sense should tell them that the money will eventually come out of their pockets, as well as ours. If the Government pays, it will come out of taxes, if from a company raising their prices. Never under estimate the stupidity of a segment of our population.

The following statement was made by Kenneth W. Stollitt, a very wise man, "There are certain truths that are true no matter how much we may deny them. In the economic realm, for instance, you cannot legislate the poor into independence by legislating the wealthy out of it. You cannot multiply wealth by dividing it. Government cannot give to people what it first does not take away from people and that which one receives without working for, another man must work for without receiving."

We would like to think that we have seen the worst of it with the payments to the Indians, the Japanese, the Holocaust victims, the Mexicans, the black farmers, the woman who split coffee on her private parts, millions to the dumb smokers who got cancer, billion dollar fees to the lawyers in the tobacco case, with probably worse to come.

Ahead, a suit against gun makers, against the fast food industry by fat slobs, suits by slavery descendants, by some 911 survivors against the Saudi and Sudanese governments over the loss of a life in boy friend, and probably some that we can't imagine.

At the risk of up setting your stomach we have learned, Medicare has shelled out nearly twenty million dollars for 31,953 penile implants with the explanation that Medicare pays for a "failure of a body part." And inflatable, a full time semi-rigged, and a multi component complete with pump, cylinders, and/or reservoir. Wouldn't that cock your pistol? Looks like a lot of pistols have been cocked. As an old time Congressman from Crockett used to say, "It's enough to make a mule throw up."

Today you can sue for anything no matter how ridiculous. I was talking to some people the other day and said that I had always wanted to be six feet tall and weigh one hundred eighty pounds. There was a lawyer present and he said in jest that he could probably fine some one to sue for this. I wouldn't be surprised. There are more stupid things than this going on in our legal system. Join the crowd.

The Renaissance

The Renaissance has been defined as a new birth or a revival. In Europe during the 14th, 15th & 16th, centuries it marked the transition from the medieval to the modern world. In Crockett and Houston County it marked the change from pre-war to post war life in this County where we live. This is not the story of an organization but a story of people. People who realized that change was needed and that it had to begin with a change in attitudes.

Houston County had seen more than half its population leave during World War II with most of them being young people. The family farms had gone with the wind, aided by progress. There was the friction between people who lived in town and those in the country, the fruit from seeds sown by self serving politicians decades ago. Mistrust between Blacks and Whites, jealously between the different towns in the County, apathy, disinterest, disgust, and just about ever other negative feeling know. This had to change.

This problem was not unique to Houston county but applied to most all of rural East Texas. Texas A&M University realized this problem and organized a ten County East Texas Development Organization that included Houston County. Tupelo, Miss., had a development program going that had proved very successful and a group from Houston County decided to see what they had done in Tupelo.

It has been my policy not to reveal full names in some of my trivia but in this case I think the names should be mentioned as a tribute to the men and women who had the vision and the will to bring these changes about. On this trip was Philip Nix, one of the effective County Agents we have ever had: R.C. (Bob) Overstreet, local hardware store owner, and Marcus Mason, County School Superintendent, and President of the Crockett Chamber of Commerce. They came back really impressed with what Tupelo had accomplished and spread the word. It was decided that a larger group representing the whole County should go see this Tupelo Program.

I think some of you younger listeners and readers will be surprised and should be impressed when you learn who took the time and spent their money to go on this charter plane trip to Miss. They were George McLean, First National Bank; John Lewis, Publisher of the Courier, Sam Arledge, local Sinclair Oil dealer, and member of the board of The Trinity River Authority, Ben Satterwhite, Satterwhite Wholesale Grocery Supply, John Merriwether, Manager 7- J Stock Farm, J. B. Sallas, Attorney and Mayor of Crockett, H. B. (Mutt) Knox, Knox Furniture Store, R. L. Barrett, Manager of East Texas Production Credit Assoc., Raymond Cornelius, Owner Crockett Hotel, C. W. Kennedy, Attorney, Jack Beasley, Jr. Davy Crockett Savings & Loan, Wilse Hail, Manager Texas Power & Light Co, J. B. McDuff, owner of the Telephone Co., C. N. (Buck) Sullivan, Sullivan Motor Co., Dale Leediker, Manager United Gas Co. Jim Gibbs, owner K.I.V.Y. radio station, Jim Rector, President Crockett State Bank, Albert K. Daniels, County Judge, and R.C. (Bob) Overstreet,

These people and this trip was the Genesis of the Houston County Development Foundation.

As soon as this group returned they began to set up a County wide organization which was called the Houston County Development Foundation. It included every incorporated town and every community in Houston County.

The first board of directors included: <u>Crockett</u> – James A. Rector, Rolland Smith, J. B. McDuff, R. C. Overstreet, C. N. Sullivan, C. L. Edmiston and H. B. Knox; <u>Grapeland</u> – John W. Kennedy, Ira Rails and M. E. Darsey, Jr, <u>Lovelady</u>- Glover LaRue and Jimmie King, <u>Kennard</u> – Roy Julian, <u>Ratcliff</u> – L. O. Killion, <u>Glover</u> – <u>Weches</u> Frank Beathard, <u>Tri-Community</u> E. E. Dickey, <u>Pennington</u> - V. O. Walker, <u>Porter Springs</u> - Grady Grounds, Jr. <u>Austonio</u> – J. B. Coon<u>, Latexo</u> – Grover Shanks, <u>Weldon</u> – Leslie Parker, and Phillip Nix, at large. The first President was James A. Rector.

This board immediately went to work meeting with the leaders of every community in the County resulting in each one forming their own chamber of commerce which was called a community council. The council members paid dues to the County organization which in turn refunded 20% back to the individual council to use as they pleased. This was a ground breaking achievement which had never been attempted before or since. Each council elected their own officers and adopted their program of work. Then things began to happen and happen fast. Changes came about. The physical things are obvious. What brought these physical changes about we will discuss in another article.

Houston County Development
Foundation - Continued

In our last discussion we reviewed how the Houston County Development foundation came into being, was organized, and started to work. The order of business was to organize the County into workable units. This was done by each community forming their own Chamber of Commerce and calling it a Community Council. I think it should be understood that time and space and the limited ability of this writer will limit the details of this effort and the credit that should be given to everyone who worked so hard to bring this about.

I think the scope of the Foundations efforts can be seen in the standing committee that were organized and the number of people involved. At one point in the Foundation's program of work there were over two hundred people through out the County involved in the following committees; Agricultural , Airport, Highway, Education, Industrial Development, Membership and Finance, Rural Community Development, Safety, Senior Citizens, Tourist Development, Trinity River, Youth Activities, Family Living, and the Houston County Water Control & Improvement District No. 1.

Working along side of these committees you had the Housing Authorities of the incorporated towns, Urban Renewal, Hospitals Authorities, and the Houston County

Planning Commission, along with The Farmers Home Administration. Back then the County Commissioners and the City Council Governments of the incorporated towns all worked together to make this program a success.

Crockett then organized the Crockett Community Council to expand the scope of the old Crockett Chamber of Commerce with a program of work to include Houston County. They had about the same committees as the County organization with some that pertained to local issues and involved almost as many people. In addition to the incorporated towns that organized almost every community in the County, they did likewise including even the smallest such as Beria, Center Grove, Cedar Branch, Halls Bluff, Mt. Zion, Post Oak, Tadmore, and Wheeler Springs

The emphasis was not only to improve our communities but also self improvement. The then popular Dale Carnegie course on "How to Win Friends and Influence People" was enthusiastically embraced with seventy five from the County completing the course. They included farmers, bankers, teachers, housewives, store clerks, you name it and they ranged in age from teenagers to grandparents. That was something to see that is unlikely to be seen again. This was an effort to change attitudes which was the common goal of all both Black and White.

Probably the most gratifying result of this whole affair was the spirit of cooperation that existed between the Black and White citizens of the County. This came from the heart and not a government decree so unlike the "in your face attitude" that exist today whereby unqualified people are elected to public office based not on their qualifications but on the color of their skins. It is a sad state of affairs whereby nobody wins.

I think everyone of the past generation can see where we have come from with the results that we see today both good and bad. We worked hard for what we defined as progress. Progress has brought us employment for our young people, good medical facilities, good water supply, good communications, a library, shopping centers, fast food stops, good fire and police protection, a school system that is struggling to keep up, at least one television in every home, not only the dream of a car for every family, but a car for each member of the family, churches of every denomination available to our people, and last but not least a modern airport.

Since life is not a bed of roses we know we have the downside of this good life. Everyone owning a car has caused traffic congestion, we are seeing more crime, a generation of children who spend their time in front of a television with no parent supervision, neighbors not knowing neighbors, and among other things a whole generation getting fatter and fatter based on their lifestyle.

We might have given the impression that every attempt to create jobs was a success so lets list some that didn't make it. An oil mill, cotton compress, five cotton gins, hardwood flooring mill, two saw mills, chair factory, baseball bat factory, archery bow factory, fishing worm farm, alfalfa dehydrating mill, two feed mills, mobile home mfg., two candy plants, pre-stressed concrete plant, furniture mfg. plant, a business form mfg. plant, and three surviving car dealerships out of thirteen that existed at one time.

We know that we can look back but can't go back which is probably a good thing. I see where the Houston County Area Chamber of Commerce is trying to accomplish what the H.C.D.F. did a generation ago. Back then it was successful because the need was there. If the need is there today they should accomplish much. The people who are trying to do something deserve all the credit.

Bird Hunting

November is bird hunting time all over the Country and for East Texas bird hunting don't mean hunting for doves, ducks, geese, turkeys, or any birds of that kind it means hunting for quail. Now in Houston County until about the 1970's it meant going after quail almost anywhere you wanted to hunt. They were that plentiful and you could cross most fences without worrying about getting permission.

Back then a lot of people had bird dogs and most of them ran loose around the neighborhood and if you knew the owner wasn't going hunting you could just jump one in the trunk of you car and take off hunting. Now back then dogs were not that hard to keep if you didn't worry about worms, rabies, running fits, occasional mange, and other things we spend money on today. Speaking of running fits you don't hear about it these days. They were really harmless except a dog would scare somebody who wasn't used to it. They would start barking, frothing at the mouth, chasing their tail and would usually seek a dark place to hide. After a while they would snap out of it and be as good as before. We have learned today that it was a lack of protein in their food that caused this condition. Back then most dog owners fed their dog's table scraps. When there was not enough table scraps we would boil cornmeal with bacon grease in it. We are told today that there was a lack of protein in that diet that caused the fits.

I have often wondered why we didn't have running fits because we ate the same thing.

Back about the time I first spoke about, small farms had started to disappear and large farms started converting to pine trees and grass and quail can't live on pine trees and grass so they started disappearing until today it is rare to find a wild covey in our County. Some people blame it on fire ants which may have some effect but it is mostly because that they don't have anything to eat.

Back then all you needed was a good close working bird dog, a shot gun and a good pair of legs, along with being a pretty good shot to bring home a limit of birds. Bird dogs were not hard to come by back then. You could usually come by a puppy from someone that you could train. If you were lucky you might find a starved bird dog among the mongrels gathered around a farm house that you could pickup for a few dollars and in many cases these made good bird dogs because they had trained themselves on the plentiful quail around them.

To someone who has the patience and ability a bird dog is not that hard to train. It is born with a nose thousands of time better than the human nose and it is born with the genes to recognize the scent of a quail out of all the other scents and stop when they smell it. There are three basic commands in training, here, whoa, and fetch. I am not here to tell you that all bird dogs are the same. Some make it and many don't. It was harder to train a dog back then because you didn't have the tools of today to do it with. If a dog made a mistake he needed to be punished right then before he forgot what he as being punished for and a dog with any sense wasn't going to keep coming back to you to be punished, so some hard headed dogs were rewarded with some number nine shot sprinkled on their back sides.

We have always had many good shots in Houston County and I am going to mention those that I have heard about knowing that I am going to miss some that should be mentioned. Dan McLean, Jimmy McLean's , grandfather, was a noted wing shot, J.D. Long, of Porter Springs was very seldom beaten, Grady Earle Pennington was know as an excellent shot in the Grapeland area, as well as J.B. Lively in that area. Bud Shivers of Crockett could bust every walnut you threw in the air with a twenty two rifle, and there are young ones today who are excellent shots.

I will finish this article with an amusing but true quail story. I used to travel and one day at a farm house in Alto I saw a young bird in a bird cage. I asked what it was and lady said that nobody seemed to know. She said her son jumped a covey of quail one day and this chick couldn't keep up and he caught it. She let me bring it to Crockett where it went on display at Sherrods and Parkers on the square. Nobody could identify the thing including the local Game Warden so I took it back to Alto. Some time later I was back at the farm and asked the lady did they ever find out what the thing was. She pointed it out to me in the yard and it was a banty rooster. A banty hen had laid an egg in a quails nest and the mamma quail hatched it.

Next time where the birds are, hunting rigs, and hunting stories.

MORE HUNTING STORIES

We talked about how bird hunting used to be in East Texas when you could pickup a bird dog almost anywhere, for very little money, go outside the City limits, and bring home a mess of quail, where they were usually cleaned and eaten that night. Back when our dogs ate what we ate got sick and most times got well on their own. Back then you might take a dog to one of our "Horse and Cow Doctors" to get a rabies shot or had to be sewed up but they sure didn't depend on treating dogs and cats for their living.

Back then, you depended on a good pair of legs, one or two close working dogs, a shot gun, and a hunting coat. When you see some of today's hunting rigs you are looking at big money. You will see a late model SUV, pulling a rigged up jeep, with a shiny dog trailer behind that. In the dog trailer will be six to twelve bird dogs of different breeds with many of them costing $2,000.00 as puppies, many having been trained by a professional trainer, with a years expense of feed, medicine, and Vet care in them. There will be several Electronic dog collars in the trailer with a remote transmitter that sends an electric shock to the errant dog. These things have several different settings on them depending on how hard the dogs head is. A low setting works for most dogs, but the setting goes strong enough to make a dog sing the Star Spangled Banner if you want him to.

I know of five or six of these rigs here in Crockett plus many more that we run into. One of the Crockett hunters has the ultimate hunting rig. He has a shiny dog trailer with six or eight dogs pulled by a Caddy Esplanade. The dogs point, he gets out shoots, the dog bring him the bird, he gets back in the air conditioned Esplanade, listened to the sweet music as he rides waiting for the dogs to point again. I know of six or eight strings of bird dogs here in Crockett comprising some forty to fifty bird dogs.

These hunters will go where the quail are. South Texas has always been where the birds were, but many hunters are hunting in North Texas where the lease prices are not so high and of course the rattle snakes are not as plentiful as in the South Texas brush country. I will tell you some true rattlesnake tales later on. In addition to the dog and dog equipment expense you can expect to spend several thousand dollars per hunter on a good bird lease. There ain't nothing cheap about it any more.

Now for you wives if some of your husbands tell you that their SUVs are on loan from the automobile makers, that the rigged up Jeeps are old WWII jeeps that didn't cost much, that the dog trailer was on loan from Jones Trailer for him to advertise for them, that the dogs from the famous Elhew and Ferrell Miller kennels are only loaned to them for publicity, and the West Texas land owners let him hunt on the land for public relations, that the dog food makers, furnish them dog food for their endorsement, and that they are furnished free shot gun shell, then you certainly should believe them. And as you believe this story you should be sure that you put your tooth under your pillow if you want the Tooth Fairy to visit.

Bird Dogs & Snakes

Knowing the risk that you might learn more about bird hunting than you wanted to, I want to relate some experiences I have had with bird dogs and snakes, some here in East Texas, some in North Texas but mostly in South Texas where you find most of the rattlesnakes. I did kill a big rattler here in Crockett one time out on the Old Madisonville highway in front of the Dr. Dean House. It was a Cane break rattler. There used to be some rattlers reported in the river bottoms that were called Timber rattlers. They and the Cane breaks might have been the same species.

Most East Texas dog's snake bites were usually by Copperheads which didn't do much damage. I once saw one of my dogs get bitten by a Copperhead. I remember his head began to swell before we got home and he didn't eat all his feed but was okay the next day.

The young Crockett hunters started hunting in South Texas when they first started hunting together, switched to North Texas and then back to South Texas when they got a ten section lease close to Cotulla on the Frio River. Now this territory had lots of Rattlesnakes. You sure had to watch where you walked especially at night.

In my last article I mentioned many of the amenities that the hunters have today like hunting rigs, electronic dog collars, and such that we never dreamed of back when we hunted. You can add to these electronic beepers on the dog's collar that emits a measured beep when the dog is moving but a continuous beep when he stops to point. Now it don't take a genius to figure out why so many covey's flush wild today, what with the beepers going full blast, a jeep pulling right up to the dogs, the hunters hollering whoa to the dogs, and no cover on the ground, the smart birds will get the heck out of there. In addition to the beepers the hunters had to have snake proof leggings and the dogs had to have boots to cope with the grass burrs.

Now an East Texas dog isn't born fearing Rattlesnakes so he must have this fear put in him and a way was provided to not only make him fear snakes but also another way to spend money. This is done at a preseason snake proofing party put on by an expert at the job. He would bring the big Rattlesnakes with the first one with no fangs and his rattles taped up. The dog with an electronic collar on, set on high would be led up to the snake. When he tried to smell it would receive the full force of the shock. He was then led around to a snake with fangs and his rattles. A broke dog upon smelling and hearing the snake would almost pull the man down who held the lead rope. If he didn't do this he was put through the whole process again. It was supposed to work. I know of at least one exception where it didn't.

My son Jim had an old dog named Ace that had been given to him. Nobody knew how old Ace was but figured he was almost old enough to vote. He had trained a many a young dog and young hunter. Well any how old Ace got the de-snaking job done on him before we went to South

Texas. One day Jim and Stanley Maxwell killed a big rattler and old Ace heard the shot and came running up. They didn't know that there was another big rattler right behind them but Ace found him and was bitten on the face. Probably old Ace just got careless but the better story is that he sacrificed himself to save Jim and Stanley. At any rate his head swelled up so bad that you couldn't tell what he was. We put him in a room and propped a door against it. The next morning Ace was out sitting on the jeep ready to hunt. His head was still swollen but he was ready to hunt. It has long been known in that Country that an animal bitten on the head will recover. Any other place will kill them. Don't know if it would work on a man. Our hunters never laid down on one.

Other than man, rattle snakes have two mortal enemies and that is the Bull snake and the Blue Indigo which can grow to ten or twelve feet long and eat the biggest rattler. Many years ago our Crockett hunters one day heard a loud commotion beside a trail and went over and found a huge Indigo that had a big rattler half swallowed with his back half rattling furiously. They said there was blood everywhere from the rattlers bites on the Indigo. Lucky for the Indigo he is immune from the rattlers venom.

The boys have killed many rattle snakes but another incident comes to mind, one that I have related in an earlier article but it illustrates some of the experiences that we have had. We were hunting on a lease near Dilley, Texas one day when we flushed a covey and a single lit off by its self. A young dog ran out and pointed it. One of the hunters went out to take the skillet shot and found the bird in the firm grip of a four foot rattler. The bird must have lit right on top of the snake. The young dog was still firmly on point. She is still in Carroll Sullivan's kennel here in Crockett.

Catching snakes is big business in South Texas. We used to watch as a buyer came every Sunday afternoon to buy snakes for the natives. It was quite a sight to see. He had a market for them from dog trainers, collectors, for their venom, skins, and for their flesh. It is supposed to be quite tasty. I served some one time at camp and every one enjoyed it until they found out what it was. The dogs enjoyed it.

A MEMORABLE TRIP

As we get older we catch ourselves thinking back to the long ago, and thinking about either how good it used to be or how bad it used to be compared to today. We know that watermelon and pork sausage was better back then and we think that sugar cane was better although we don't know how it is today because we can't chew it. We compare our ailments of today with those of yesterday and know the cures are much better today. Speaking of ailments I had the stomach bug, for want of a better name, just before Xmas and I thought it was the worst case that I had ever had until I remembered one I had over fifty years ago and in another Country.

Just before I was discharged from the service in 1946, I checked into a hospital in El Paso to get some work done on my face. I was in a car wreck during the war and managed to put my face through a car wind-shield. Because of the glass in my face, and the fact that it was three days before they could find a sober Army doctor to work on me, they didn't do a very good job on my face resulting in my having to go to a hospital in El Paso to have some patch work done on it. So before I came to Crockett an old Uncle of mine who lived in San Angelo offered to take me on a trip to Mexico.

We fished on the way down where the little Mexican boys stole every fish we caught, listened to eighty thousand Mexicans cheering the bull fighters, saw poor peasants crawling over cobblestone streets to light a candle and leave their hard earned money at the Altar of the Catholic Church, and got a Mexican parking ticket which caused our license plate to be removed. A very effective enforcement. A small bribe took care of the problem, back to my story.

We were staying at a nice small two story hotel with no elevators that served family style meals. One afternoon while wandering around seeing the sights, I got hungry and ate a sandwich at a small bar. Well that night sitting in the lobby my sins caught up with me and I got sick. Like a sick dog who wants to crawl under the house I tried to make it to my room. Needless to say I couldn't make it. Soon I heard a soft knock at my door and there stood a small porter with a mop, rags and a bucket. I apologized and tipped him and received some of the best advice that I have ever received. He said: "Senor next time you get sick, stand still." I have always remembered this and during my Xmas spell I tried to stand still.

When we left Mexico City we decided to take a scenic short cut back to Texas and it was then that I had one of the strangest and most moveable experiences that I have ever had. We had long passed any paved roads and instead of bridges, we were crossing streams on hand drawn ferries and although we wouldn't admit we were lost, we sure didn't know where we were. We stopped at a little sun baked village to get some lunch and to ask directions. We had no sooner gotten out of the car before a crowd of natives gathered around us shouting Americana, Americana, and almost pulling us down the street. I failed to mention that I was still in my American army uniform having had no chance to buy civilian clothes. They looked like they meant us no harm so we followed them. They knocked on a door and an American woman opened the door. I shall never forget the look on her face and she probably didn't soon forget the look on mine. She looked haggard and all used up and when we got inside we found out why, lying on the bed was her husband who at first glance showed he was in the advanced stage of alcoholism. He could hardly raise his head. We found out that he was a decorated American Officer with a Purple Heart ribbon on his uniform. He insisted on getting dressed and taking us to lunch. He had to have a drink before he could even get dressed and his wife had to help him with that. As a result of talking with her out of ear shot of him, we learned that they had been in this village since the war ended and she could not get him to go back to the States. He would go as far as the Border to get his check and then they would return to this village.

We had a pleasant enough visit and then we had to go. My Uncle and I felt a great sadness for them, especially when she asked us to contact her parents and tell them she was okay and she would stay with him and keep trying to get him home. I have always wondered if they ever got back to the States. I know one thing I made sure that I never went back down there.

THE SOUND OF TAPS

We have heard the beautiful and haunting sound of taps being played lately, especially last Memorial Day. Like all tunes that are played on an Army bugle it is composed of only four notes. During my time of Army service it was played on only two occasions, at ten P.M. that signaled lights out, and when a comrade was laid to rest. When I volunteered for service in November of 1940, I let it slip that I had learned to blow a bugle in Grade School and that did it. I became a bugler in Uncle Sam's Army.

All it takes to blow a bugle is strong lips and cheek muscles and plenty of hot air so really all I had to develop was the lips and cheek muscles having been then, as now blessed with the hot air. I was provided with a bugle and a record of all the bugle calls and there was a bunch of them. I couldn't then and still cannot read a note of music so they had to be committed to memory. Back before radio and telephones this was the chief means of communication.

The first call of the day was Reveille, which woke them up, then Mess Call, Assembly, to call the roll, Sick Call, Mail Call, if it was payday there was a call for that. There were special calls like Attention, Charge, like John Wayne used to do, Recall, which meant for John to get the heck out of there. Then the next regular call was Tattoo, the beautiful and hardest to master, which was played at nine at night which was the signal for everyone to settle in and get ready for Taps at Ten when the lights went out.

After more than sixty years I can still remember the feeling I experienced, when as a young country boy far from home, I stood alone under the stars and blew Taps. That was nothing compared to the sensation that I experienced when I played Taps for a Military Funeral. A comrade of ours was killed and his funeral was held in a remote rural cemetery. A squad of men and I were assigned to do the Military honors. The program called for the preacher to conclude his part, then the squad would fire the rifles, and then I, who was in the background, would play Taps. Everything went smoothly until the Preacher finished, but when the rifles went off the widow screamed loud enough to wake the dead and everyone almost went into shock, especially me. My mouth was so dry I could not have wet a postage stamp. I finally composed myself and got it done. Thank God I never had to do that again.

The bugle long ago was replaced by the trumpet and recorded bugle calls. The trumpet is far superior to the old bugle because of its range and better tone. Harry James, in my estimation, the greatest trumpet player of my generation, proved what could be done with a trumpet when he played the "The Flight of the Bumble Bee" on a trumpet in concert in Carnegie Hall. He would have made a terrific bugler. That may have been how he got started.

As beautiful as Taps is, it can be more appreciated when you know the words that go with it. They go like this:

> Day is done, Gone the Sun
> From the hills, From the Plains
> From the Sky, All is well,
> Safe at rest, God is nigh

Bob Mattox

Isn't that beautiful? By the way, the eternal question has been since the bugler wakes every one else up, who wakes the bugler up? The Corporal of the guard wakes him. Who wakes the Corporal of Guard? Maybe the Sergeant. Who wakes the Sergeant? Who knows. We did have alarm clocks back then, maybe that's what got them all up.

Good Old Days?

I have people ask me quite often what it was like in the old days. Of course the so called old days could go on back to the Civil War and beyond but they really mean back to the days of the great depression that I grew up in. It is hard for me to believe that so few of us are left that experienced this.

Chester Hines is renovating an old house and passed some old business records on to me from that period. I thought I would share with you some of the prices some sixty five years ago and some Crockett Citizens who traded with this business and others like it and who with, maybe with a few exceptions, are all gone. It was interesting to me to read these names that I could identify with and I thought it might be of interest to you.

Water bill $1.00, sewerage $1.00, movie ten cents, butter 37 cents, 1# Hamburger 5 cents, coffee 2# 35 cents, one qt. paint $1.55, E.V. Allbright, C. Lochfield, B.F. Chamberland, W.D. Julian, Mrs. W.H. Denny, W.D. Collins, J.D. Robbins, N.O. Routledge, W.P. Bishop, W. C. Shivers, Mrs. S.W. Craddock, Leo Knox, Mrs. Dent, J.H. Crow, Joe Brannen, Mrs. Cecil Bryce, Gude Bly School, J. L. Dean Jr., P. Caprielian.

Light Bill $3.89, Doctors house visit $2.50, 25# ice 15 cents, # cheese 23 cents, hair cut 25 cents, # tomatoes 6 cents. J.S. Corley, Mrs. J. Spence, Vernon Garner, Edgar

Houston, A.A. Scott, J. Buttry, M. McConnell, S.M. Monzingo, Bly Jones, Walter Hazlett, W.E. Wilcox, Carter Ramey, Mrs. Jim Porter, Smith Baughman, Len Bromberg, J.H. Reinche, J.F. Mangum, Lee Smith, Charlie Stockton, J. Murray, Ed Burton, Mrs. J.B. Stanton, R.L. Allee, F.M. Myers, R. Heard, Howard Wooten.

United Gas bill $2.80, gallon under coating $1.35, pint milk 5 cents, big Baby Ruth or Butterfiner candy bars 3 for 10 cents. Mrs. F.A. Smith, W.K. McLean, Mrs, J.D. Glenn, Tom Moore, C.W. Jones, J. D. Woodard, Leonard May, S.D. Farkley, Mrs. Boone, Carl Morrow, Dock Beavers, Page Hale, G.E. McLean, T. Van Pelt, E.D. Burton, Travis Moore, Stokes Dean, T.D. Craddock, E.C. Langrum.

Box rent 60 cents, catsup 10 cents bottle, new Ford or Chevy $750.00, gasoline 15 cents a gallon, E. Caprielian, Mrs. Louise Miles, May McLean, W. E. Hale, Jr., Clyde Douglas, Anna Austin, Dan Callahan, Mrs. Fulgham, C. Willis, C. W. Butler, Bob Greene Minni Craddock, W. J. Sexton, A. H. Parrish, Lena Klein, Byrde Wooters, W. D. Dudley, G. B. Lake, Ellis Sexton, Johnny McConnell, the Schmidt house, H. Temple, Mrs. Jordon, Lee Beavers, Mrs. F. A. Smith, S.H. Woodley, Mrs. Driskell, Mrs. Powers, F. M. Boone, V. B. Tunstall, Willie Jordon, W. B. Bryce, Ben E. Smith, J. S. Caskey, Beth Wedemeyer, W. E. Shivers, Rudd Spinks, J. W. Shivers, Nannie English, T. E. Walden, J. W. Moore, H. J. Trube, J. K. Maxwell, Dee Jones, Herman Ainsworth, G. H. Henderson, A. O. Hooper, C. Neel, C. L. Hooks, T. J. Ham, C. A. Carpenter, Harry Rankin, A. Rush, H. R. Baldree, C. D. Towery.

Skilled labor 30 cents an hour, unskilled 10 cents and hour, eggs 29 cents doz., cigarettes 15 cents per pack, stamps 2 cents each, telephone $2.00 month. D. D. Gentry, David Gipson, E. R. Keels, Mrs. John Lingold, Ada Johnson, Clifton O'Neil, Loretta Halyard, R. C. Lloyd, J. W. Arledge, Mrs. Hortense Sweet, Mrs. Evelyn Rice, Mozell King, Mrs. John Spence, E. D. Houston, L. L. Murray, H. J. Phillippo, and T. J. Waller.

This is but a small sample of the prices and the customer of a small business a generation ago. Some will say "I wish I could buy a hamburger for a nickel." Those who bought the nickel burger worked a half hour to pay for it. Today a half hours work at minimum wage will not only buy a burger but fries and a drink. The low wage earner of that day worked an hour and a half to buy a gallon of gasoline. To day's hourly wage will buy three gallons of gas with change.

You will never see conditions like that again simply because people today will not put up with it. That was a depression as opposed today's talk of recession. There is a difference. A recession is when your neighbor is out of work. A depression is when you are out of work.

GOD BLESS AMERICA

Giving Advice

As we grow older we catch ourselves giving advice whether we are asked for it or not. It is a compliment to be asked for advice by someone but the odds that your children or grand children will ever ask your advice are greater than the odds of winning the lottery and if they took any advice you gave them it would be as great a miracle as walking on water. I understand that some parents have had this happen. It has never happened to me. Advice should be given before something happens. If given afterward it becomes hindsight and if repeated over and over it becomes preaching.

If we had been asked we could have told Custer not to split his forces at the Little Bighorn. If we had been asked we could have told the Generals how to catch Bin Laden and all his men simply by building a Wal-mart Super Center in Afghanistan and staking it out. They would have all eventually come there and we could have picked them up one by one. Speaking of Generals have you noticed how smart all our Generals have gotten since they retired? Most of them spent their twenty or thirty years not sticking their necks out and passing the buck and now they are being paid big bucks to go on television and tell our active Generals how to win the war.

We have been led to believe that the younger generation is getting smarter. Now my generation might not have had the education that young folks are getting today but we would have had enough sense not to spend our hard earned money on a lottery ticket at 28,500,000 to one odds, not to borrow money at 18 to 20 percent interest, and certainly not to believe some slime bug who says he runs a non profit organization that can cut your payments in half and get you out of debt.

All the talk of war has gotten our Country divided as to what course we should pursue. I don't know somethings you have to leave up to people who know the facts. There is one thing that I know from experience and that war leaves its mark in many ways. Some not so obvious as the loss of life and property. My experience goes back to WWII when I saw many of the National Guard troops being called up or drafted into service decide to marry their small town sweethearts and drag them off to camp with them. Many things can happen in this kind of situation and most of them are not for the best. First and foremost an enlisted man was not paid enough to keep up a wife, and Army towns back then were the pits where you would not want a wife to live much less kids, in addition, the soldier husband could get killed or wounded, also they were exposed to many opportunities, as were the wives left at home, to break their marriage vows, and lastly many came home not satisfied with what they had left. There was then a popular WWI song that went "How You Gonna Keep Them Down On The Farm After They Seen Par-ee?" Many a glamorous foreign girl has made a home sick soldier forget many things not only the farm but the bride he left at home. I have strong memories of seeing those young wives, some with children, some pregnant, some without money to get home, waving good-by to their husband heading to war. I know the sadness they suffered because it was my unpleasant task to censor their mail that they sent back home and to suffer with them. Thank goodness many, many of those marriages worked out for the best but some didn't.

Getting back to the subject of giving advice the best advice I ever received on the subject of giving advice was from a wise old man who said "When a man ask you for advice tell him what he wants to hear and he will think you are smart and will tell people how smart you are. I haven't heard my phone ringing asking my advice but in case anyone wants my advice give me time to find out something about you so I tell you what you want to hear.

ACQUIRING CULTURE

A few weeks ago I was informed that we had tickets to something to do with a quartet at the Methodist Church. I thought boy I like quartet music. Give The World a Smile Every Day, Listen Everybody From Near and Far, The Bewley Gang is Here Again , The Old Rugged Cross, and many more songs that I remembered. When I looked at the program I saw where it said String Quartet. I thought well I have always liked fiddle music and old tunes like Sally Goodin, Boil Them Cabbages, Orange Blossom Special, and many others. I settled down thinking this was going to be right up my alley.

When the program began three young men and a young woman appeared each with a fiddle of a different size. I suspected that I was in trouble when the spokesman addressed us in a very heavy French accent. The program was divided into works by different composers with four pieces by each composer. I will say this, that I never heard more beautiful music come out of violins although I could not tell the difference between one piece or another.

When I remarked that I had been trapped into something I was told it wouldn't hurt me to absorb some Culture. I got to thinking what is Culture? One definition defines it as development or improvement by education or training resulting in enlightenment or refinement resulting from such development. Since I never been educated or trained in absorbing this kind of Culture I knew I was in for a long night.

Now the young emcee explained in his accent, that I could even understand, that each series would consist of four pieces and for the audience to hold their applause until all four pieces were completed and then at his signal we could applaud. After the first piece was completed a segment of the audience displayed their Cultural training by bursting into applause therefore setting off the whole crowd. The young man again explained the procedure but to no avail there was wild applause after each piece. I saw people who understood great music applaud with a rapt look on their face and I saw some like me who had been cleaned up and dragged to the concert, and didn't know Beethoven's fifth from a fifth of Jack Daniels, who were politely applauding along with the rest.

After awhile, I realized that with my Cultural background I had about all the Culture that I could absorb in one night and it wasn't right to have more Culture wasted on me when someone else could use it. I began to figure a way to politely get out of there. I couldn't just get up and walk out and besides we came in one car. I thought back to the time of Nero, the Roman emperor who fiddled while Rome burned. His concerts were so bad, people were paid to faint so they could be carried out. I asked Peggy if she felt faint which she didn't, and then I thought that wouldn't work because I couldn't carry her if she did faint. Then I thought that I could faint but discarded that idea. About that time intermission came and since we both agreed that we might feel faint if we went back in we came on home.

Now please don't think for a minute that this piece of tomfoolery is intended to take anything away from the great music and the people who really appreciate it, or the Piney Woods Fine Arts Association who brought this program to Crockett. Thank goodness today's generation with today's Culture can appreciate music like this and should be offered more of it while excusing my generation for remember the Culture we were brought up with.

TRAFFIC ON THE SQUARE

I was at a meeting the other day where Tim Culp, the speaker, was explaining the work of the Chamber of Commerce. When the meeting was opened to questions and comments from the floor, most were concerned with traffic and parking on the Square. This really brought back memories from some fifty years ago when I was manager of the Chamber and conducted similar meetings. Although it could stand improvement, the traffic situation on the Square has improved dramatically since those early days.

If you would really like a comparison between traffic conditions today an back then, count the vehicles passing by while you are waiting to get on or off the Loop. We know we didn't have near the vehicle traffic back then as we have today, so let's say that only one vehicle out of five passing through Crockett today had to cross the Square. That was the case before the Loop was built. Crockett has always had lots of through traffic to cope with. There are obvious reasons for this. We are not called the Crossroads of East Texas for nothing, with eight major highways, and as many Farm to Market roads running through our town, and according to a recent article in the Wall Street Journal, Crockett, today is located within one hundred and fifty miles of 70% of all Texans, and within two Hundred miles of 90% of all Texans, so it is no surprise why we have today's traffic. Another contributing factor is the increase in our local traffic, which has increased from one car per family to, in some cases, one for each member of the family.

To say it was chaotic is an under statement. Before the loop, most all businesses were located on or just off the square, and as is the case today, no back alleys for loading or unloading. All the businesses gave curb service with the customers doubled parked to receive their goods. Parking was at a premium around the square. I would say that back then, the merchants were very cooperative and would never take up a parking space in front of their own business unless there was an emergency. The emergency was created when they could not fine a space to park in front of another business. Another contributing factor was back then the jail and the Sheriff's living quarters were located on the top floor of the Court house and the Sheriff, his family, and personnel, the elected officials, and all the County employees, considered it their Divine right to park around the Court House there by taking up most of those parking spaces.

Many solutions were tried and discarded including two way traffic around the square, signal lights at each approach, parking meters, Crockett's own Meter Maid who placed tickets on offenders cars who, in most cases, ignored them. A City Marshall who did his best to enforce the law. Some wag even suggested banning all parking on the square on vehicles that were not paid for. It has always been considered dangerous to drive around the square, but more so back then because the bricks that covered the square and approaches had not been covered with paving as they are now, and its undulating surface was slick when wet. Strangers have always wondered why we haven't had more wrecks on the Square. We have always joked that it is so dangerous that it is safe. In all my years here I don't remember but three fatalities on and off the Square. Back then Crockett was known for its terrible driving conditions on the Square but also the home of the best Chicken Fried Steak in Texas, served by the old Royal Café which was located smack dab in the middle of the Square.

We have other claims to fame besides the Davy Crockett thing. By the way did you know that one time Crockett got national publicity when Jefferson Davis, who owned the Crockett Democrat, presented Richard Nixon who was at a press convention in Galveston, with two coon skin caps for his daughters? I bet they still have them. Something else that we can brag about is the fact that we were the first town in Texas to ask the Highway Department to build a loop around their town, thus becoming the smallest town in Texas with a loop completely around it. When we went to Austin to ask for this, we knew we would catch a lot of flak for our actions when we got home, but we were unprepared for the fire storm it produced. Future Planners tell us that some time in the future we will need another loop further out to handle our growing traffic. If any of you young people are asked to go to Austin to ask for this, I would advise you to use an assumed name and sneak over there and back as quietly as possible and don't admit anything.

The Treasure Hunt

When I got out of the Service in 1946, and came to Crockett, I was told that I had to file and income tax return. Since neither I or any of my folks ever heard of such a thing much less filled out one, I had to have some help. Someone suggested that I see a fellow who had just returned from the War, who worked over at the court house in the Tax Collectors office. That's when I met Roy Garner. Now Roy was a character who set the pattern for all characters to follow.

Roy had grown up in Crockett finishing high school here, went to college, spent the War flying off air craft carriers, and came back here after the War. Roy was a successful business man and in doing all this, part of him never grew up. I guess I was in the same shape because I was in on most of the stuff that he came up with. Neither of us were married at the time and it's a wonder that Mary Beth Lundy and Peggy Knox ever married us.

One of our earlier episodes concerned a treasure hunt. There was a character here in Crockett named Jonah, the name being very appropriate, as you will find out later. Jonah was always telling Roy about a buried treasure that he knew about. He said a vision had come to him in a dream and he convinced Roy, which wasn't too hard to do, that he could find it but it had to be done at night.

To say Jonah was off his rocker was an understatement. Back then we didn't have psychiatrist here in Crockett to describe different stages of mental illness, so we used our own descriptions. Being a half bubble off was the first stage, then when his elevator didn't go all the way to the top was the second stage, and the last stage was when his pilot light blew out. It was plane to see that Jonah was well into the last stage.

I got a call from Roy one night telling me that we were going treasure hunting with Jonah. Said he had the shovels, lanterns, and everything we needed. I told him it was too cold to get out, much less on a fool thing like that. He added that he also had a full fifth of Walkers Deluxe whiskey. Back then that was about the best whiskey you could buy for under $5.00 a fifth. That sold me and I told him to pick me up.

When he picked me up he had Jonah and all the tools and the Walkers of which we all took a sip to ward off the chill. I remember the first sight was out the Pennington Highway in a field under a pine tree. With Jonah doing the digging Roy and I spent the time sampling the Walkers. We finally gave up that spot and tried a spot out on the Kennard Highway all this time testing the Walkers. We tried a few more spots all the time taking a few more pulls on the Walkers when Jonah decided that the signs weren't right and that we needed to try another night. By that time Roy and I would have agreed to anything.

A day or two later Jonah came by Roy's office and Roy told him the treasure had been found and dug up. Jonah got real upset and accused Roy and me of going back and getting his treasure. He said he was going to report us to the F.I.B. and that we would be in big trouble.

We never heard from Jonah or the F. I. B., but we had already decided that there probably would never be another treasure hunt, but if we ever went on another one, we would take a better grade of booze. That's just a sample of some of the fool things that Roy Garner and I pulled off. Those that can be printed I will tell you about later.

Movies of the Past

After learning that my cultural back ground in music hadn't reached the level of classical string quartet music the directors of the Piney Woods Fine Arts Association, in a generous tongue-in cheek gesture, gave me a stage door pass to the Romancing The Movies performance at the Civic Center last week. They hit the nail on the head. The sixteen piece band was great, playing the theme songs from many old movies of the past plus many more. I really enjoyed this one.

I remember the first movies that I ever saw. They were silent movies with the dialogue printed on the screen. The music was furnished by a piano player in the orchestra pit located right under the screen. I had an aunt who played for our local movie house. The musician would follow the action on the screen and play the appropriate music for each scene. For the sad scenes they would play sad music, for the love scenes romantic songs, for the chase scenes that every western movie had, they would invariable play "The William Tell Overture." When I was real young I thought the action was taking place behind the movie theater, and one day I had a chance to look back there and was disappointed when I found nothing but garbage cans and trash. That's when I first moved past the stage of make believe, Santa Claus, and the tooth fairy.

The first movie that I went to, where I still remember the title, was the original version of the movie, Ben Hur. It was in the late 1920's and I remember school turned out so we could go see it. Another all time great was "Gone With The Wind" which I saw in 1938 or 39 when it first came out. It was the first that I ever went to with an Intermission, I will never forget the reaction of some women in the audience when Rhett Butler used the word damn. Wonder what their reaction would be at one of today's movies? We have come a long way since then. A long way down, that is.

Before television, our entertainment was the movies. Looking back it seems that it was about every ten years that the industry came out with a really good one. I have mentioned, Ben Hur, the last one, then came Gone with the Wind, Mutiny on the Bounty, Casablanca, Sound of Music, Patton, Lonesome Dove, The Thorn Birds, God Father One, and surprisingly, God Father Two, Dances With Wolves, Lawrence of Arabia and many more. That's just some that I can recall and see over and over. I see some of those good ones over and over partly because I like them, but also, maybe I can understand what they say the second or third time around. I wish they made a television set where you could stop the action and keep repeating the scene until you understood what they were whispering.

The band played the theme songs from most of those old movies and many more. In hearing them you remembered the beautiful women who played in them. There was Elizabeth, Lana, Betty, Grace, Ingrid, Vivian, Marilyn, Natalie, and many others. Just about every school boy fell in love with them and their pinups adorned many high school lockers, college dormitory walls, and went to war with the soldiers in WWII. To young men of that time they had a certain mystic that put them far above the crowd. They were put on a pedestal and held in awe by those who had a schoolboy crush on them.

Today, probably the hardest thing for my generation to accept is to see the mystic stripped from the beautiful women of today as they bare their bodies in public, use gutter language, and what is really devastating is to learn that some suffer from the unglamorous medical problems that some admit publicly. Surely our beautiful heroines didn't suffer from these maladies. Or did they? If they did, I hope I never find out about it.

PACKING FOR A TRIP

Went to the 50th Wedding Anniversary party of Mary and Harold Walker awhile back where the children's gift to them was a trip to Sapporo, Japan. We went on such a trip with Mary, Harold, and their youngest daughter, Mary Jane. It was a wonderful trip.

Seasoned travelers like the Walkers will tell you to pack what you think you will need and then unpack and then discard half of what you have packed. Then do this again and you will still probably have more clothes than you will need. Contrary to all advice we did just the opposite and packed our new luggage to the brim. We had an outfit for any occasion including dinner at the Royal Palace. It was too heavy to carry so Peggy bought a fold up luggage carrier that lasted until it broke down before we boarded the plane in Dallas. All this time the Walkers sailed along with three peoples belongings packed in three small bags that Mary and Mary Jane had no trouble carrying.

From Dallas to Los Angeles, then seventeen hours on a plane to Seoul, Korea that the population of Lovelady, Smith Grove, Weldon, Pearson Chappell, and Vistula could have fitted into, we landed in Seoul, Korea. A few things that I recall about Seoul is that Peggy's coffee pot, that she never left home without, blew up when she plugged it into a DC outlet at the hotel. Then on to Bangkok, Thailand, where I saw idiots drinking snake blood supposedly to improve their manhood. I bet the snakes are glad for Viagra.

From Bangkok to Taipei, Taiwan, where a strap broke on one bag, and we lost a zipper on one bag and we threw away some clothes. On to Bali, Indonesia, where Harold and I played golf. Two very small Indonesian women, barefoot and sarongs, caddied for us. We didn't lose a ball. On to Hong Kong, where we shipped home a hundred pounds of unneeded clothes and miscellaneous items. One day in China, and off to Japan with our bags held together by ropes, we landed in Osaka, Japan. We visited a family that our son had stayed with on the Lions Club Student Exchange Program.

In Osaka we boarded the famous "Bullet Train" to Tokyo, by then dragging our luggage. You would think that the coolies that you read about in Japan would be available to carry your bags. There was no such thing in any country we visited. I can understand not wanting to carry our bags, for fear of injury, but there was no porter to carry anyone's bags. The 'Bullet Train" ride was quite an experience traveling in excess of one hundred seventy five miles per hour with very little sense of motion. Our luggage held together by rope and wire drew some stares but held together.

From Tokyo to Yokohama, back to Tokyo, then to Sapporo on the Island of Hokkaido, to where we visited friends of the Walkers. Our host took us all over the Island of Hokkaido, to Summo wrestling, and to a Geisha House, which was not much fun since Peggy, Mary, and Mary Ann went with us. All this time, I was slipping around discarding some of my extra clothes. Should have been doing the same thing with Peggy's, but didn't know where to start. Harold and I played some golf and I found out when I attempted to either buy or rent some golf shoes that the biggest shoe available on the Island was a size eight.

From Hokkaido back to Tokyo hotel where I was almost jolted out of my bed, I thought the ropes on our luggage had popped loose, but found out it was an earthquake. From Tokyo, to Hawaii, and on to Dallas where the last strap broke on our luggage when we threw it in the car. You have heard the expression of a "Trip of a Lifetime." In my case that was really true because that one trip has lasted me a lifetime.

Hindsight

Hindsight is defined in the dictionary as perception of the nature and exigencies of a case after the advent: then it goes on to say that hindsight is easier than foresight. When I was growing up hindsight was always defined as "shutting the barn door after the horse got out.

History is full of people who wish that they had done differently. Take Eve for example; you know she wished that she had not eaten the apple. After all, the Garden must have been full of other goodies that she could have chosen. I bet the Serpent wished she hadn't done it.

Noah had to have been sorry that he took that pair of fire ants aboard the Ark. Lots wife just had to look back on their flight from Sodom and was turned into a pillar of salt. Lot might have been glad, but you know she wasn't.

George Washington, known as the father of our Country, should have taken better care of his teeth and not been stuck with false teeth. They were made of wood you know. Did you ever wonder why he was never caught smiling? This writer has the same regrets as George did.

Custer probably wouldn't have split his forces at the battle of Little Bighorn causing his defeat. Sam Houston wouldn't have taken that big bite of hot sweet potato at a formal dinner, and spit it out on the table with the excuse "that only a damned fool would have swallowed that." Davy Crockett would have probably stayed in Tennessee with his wife and children instead of dying in Texas.

Moving right along; We know Nixon regretted Water Gate as did Clinton for dallying with that young woman, at least getting caught. If Dan Quayle had it to do over he would have learned how to spell potato before he refereed the spelling match, and so on.

Hindsight would surely have kept us out of some unpopular wars. And to put it in Sam Houston's words, "Only damned fools would have let our Country get flooded with foreigners." Of course Congress is going to solve this problem by giving them legal papers. We took Texas from the Mexicans with guns and they are going to take it back by having kids and voting.

Of course, until the end of time we are going to continue beating the old dead horse about slavery. It was wrong at the time and it is just as wrong today to continue to blame a race of people who absolutely had nothing to do with it.

I guess the champion late barn door shutters, would have to be Congress. In order to justify their existence they spend billions of our tax dollars investigating things of the past and most of the time having nothing to show for it. The mentality of some in that August Body is best revealed in the words uttered by Rep. Bill Janklow; the speed demon who killed the fellow on the motorcycle, when he said that although he still suffers from memory loss and confusion, he can still carry on his duties in Congress. They should elect him Speaker of the House.

I guess if you had to have a contest and give a prize for the best "Wish I could do it over again" it would have to be for a man who either doesn't care that hell has no fury like that of a woman scorned, and goes ahead and cheats on his wife and gets himself caught. The old saying is; "to err is human, to forgive is divine." Now it doesn't say anything about forgetting. Old experienced hands will tell you that when it comes to memory; a woman can put an elephant to shame. Some who have suffered say retribution can go on for the rest of your life, slapping you in the face when you least expect it. Men can do some dumb things but that takes the prize.

Some think that someday Congress will run out of something to do and will open and investigation of the Crucifixion in order to fix blame. My lawyer, Loophole Lewinsky, says it will be the Romans or the Jews and he can make a case either way. Who knows, crazier things have happened in this Country.

Pigeons

For quite awhile I have been noticing a large flock of pigeons flying around the square. I figured that some pigeon fancier was just releasing them for their daily exercise as most breeders do, but lately, I have been seeing them all through the day sitting on the downtown buildings. That could become bad news. If they get started nesting on these buildings we will wish that we had never heard of a pigeon. They multiply like rats and not only mess up building, streets, and Easter Bonnets, they carry parasites and disease. I understand that they already have a foot hold at the Civic Center. Many of the large Cities are having to pay to have them trapped because of the mess that they create.

There are many breeds of pigeons, some of which I have raised in my younger days. I have had Pouters, Fan Tails, Tumblers, and Homers, which look like the ones who are taking up residence on the square. The most entertaining pigeons were the ones my boys had when they were young and those were the Tumblers. When you turned them out they would gain altitude and then begin to turn backward flips one after another almost to the ground. My boys never tired of watching them.

Probably the pigeon best known to the layman is the Homing Pigeon. You transport one hundreds of miles from its loft and it will return. Breeders hold many races where the fastest bird can earn lots of money. Some come straight home, some get lost, some stop and rest, which might explain why some in the country will have one stop for a few days in their barn and then move on.

This homing trait which has never been fully explained has caused these birds to be used as messengers in war with the earliest account being the siege of Troy. They have been used in every war up until WWII with extensive use in WWI when they provided the difference between victory and defeat. The Signal Corps had pigeons at the beginning of WWII and may still have. We used some in the early days of WWII but for no serious purpose.

My Maternal uncle, who raised pigeons all his life, wrote and article right after the end of WWI about the part that Homing Pigeons played in that bloody conflict. With no radios and the primitive telephone systems of that day the pigeons were the chief means of communication between headquarters and the trenches.

We have mentioned that the pigeons would always return to their loft. They used the birds that had eggs or young in the nest because they would always return or die trying. The pigeons lofts were portable so that they could move them where needed.

My uncle in his article gives some examples of the exploits of these remarkable birds. In one engagement, 72 birds were used and not one failed to return. Traveling at an average speed of 30 miles per hour, 442 pigeons delivered 443 messages safely. There was "Big Tom" with a breast wound and a leg shot off that delivered his message, as did "The Meeker" who flew 24 miles in 24 minutes with an eye shot out. "The Spike" was more fortunate but just as brave making 52 round trips from the front without a scratch. Then the most famous of all was "Cher Ami," the bird credited with saving the Lost Battalion. In spite of a serious breast wound and a leg, with the capsule on it, hanging by a ligament he made it, there by saving the Battalion. The Signal Corps honored him by bringing him back to America where he stands on one leg in a glass case in our National Museum.

I have raised pigeons all my life starting out with just common birds and I used to enjoy just watching them in the loft and in their graceful flight but, I don't enjoy seeing them on our public buildings knowing the mess that they are going to make.

BITS AND PIECES

Much to my and others surprise I have out lived another pickup. It's been so long since I bought one I had forgotten how much the procedure has changed. Used to you were given the price of the vehicle and you made your choice.

Now you are given the monthly payment on each one because with low interest almost every buyer is on the "forever" payment plan. I recently asked a friend who had just bought a new truck what it cost. He said he didn't even ask the price he just told them what he could pay each month and to go from there.

You will always say that you just want a plain vanilla truck with no frills or gadgets but you will end up with most of them. Our guardian protectors in Washington, in their efforts to keep us alive to pay taxes have mandated that each vehicle have seat belts with a bell that drives you nuts until it is fastened, an air bag that will blow up in your face at the least bump, a buzzer that will remind you to take your keys out whether you want to or not, remote door keys that blow the horn for whatever reason, and doors that lock when the engine starts. Now most of this is on the plain vanilla truck that I got. On top of all this is a light that flashes "thief" every time I get in the thing.

There is so much new information and gadgets coming out each year and we are so far behind. I am having trouble just writing this article on this confounded computer.

After many years we still do not know how to turn off the flashing time clock on the VCR, or how to work the satellite system that was given to us, or even set the time on one of those clocks with no hands. Oh well who wants to catch up anyway.

On a more serious note I noticed that deer season kicked off Saturday. You could tell by the people missing in church, Sunday. For over forty years I never missed a season opener.

Serious hunters will arrange everything including child birth in order to make opening week, leaving many a deer hunting widow to manage for herself. One such long suffering wife described the feelings of many in the following poem.

The Hunter: Behold the hunter. He riseth early in the morning

> And disturbeth the whole household. Mighty are
>
> His preparations. He goes forth full of hope and
>
> When the day is spent, he returneth smelling of
>
> Strong drink and the truth is not in him.

Deer are quite plentiful in our County now but this was not always the case. Up until the last few years hunters who wanted to get a deer usually went to the Hill Country where you could see more deer in one morning that you could see in Houston County in a season.

A turn around started in 1955 when the Game Department released two truck loads of deer in the County. One that I witnessed was at the Shady Grove Fire Tower and another near Weches. The season was closed for five years and with a change in attitude of meat hunters the deer population took off from there.

Today with reasonable effort you can expect to kill a good deer that in most cases is almost twice the size of the Hill Country deer with a better rack of horns.

It's refreshing to see that some government programs can work. This is a shinning example.

Back When

Among all the things that a merciful Creator placed here on earth for his children, corn would have to rate right at the top. Corn and its derivatives have contributed to man's survival almost since he appeared on earth. It has been found in ancient tombs and played a big part in the Jamestown Colony's early survival when the Indians taught them how to raise it. The Indians showed the people how to fertilize it the natural way by burying a fish in the ground and planting a corn seed above it.

Our forefathers depended primarily on corn, sweet potatoes, pork, collard greens when available, and syrup to make the winters on. This was supplemented with what wild game that could be taken. Corn could be used in so many different ways. It could be parched, boiled for hominy, fed to live stock, but its greatest benefit was when it was ground into meal and baked, it creates a dish "fit for the Gods" as my old Uncle used to say when he ate my mothers corn bread, and indeed when crumbled up in a glass of sweet milk or buttermilk it was a meal in itself that is hard to beat.

The lack of eggs or milk made little difference in eyes of those country cooks when it came to making bread because that called for the creation of another delight and that was hot water cornbread which is still one of my favorites. It goes by many names, corn pone which is baked in one large piece, hoe cakes, dog bread, and maybe others, but I have always identified it as a patty made from corn meal, salt, sugar, boiling water and fried in grease. It was so good anyway you ate it, from the skillet, cold along with a fresh onion after school, eaten from a hunting sack on a bird hunt, soaked in turnip green or purple hull pea juice, and above all else, with fresh cow butter and ribbon cane syrup poured all over it. It also made a wonderful cold weather breakfast when made into mush with fresh butter, sugar and milk added.

I have mentioned dog bread. Back when I was growing up there were always dogs around to be fed. Back then we didn't know what store bought dog food was and even if we had known, there was no money for such a thing. They were fed table scraps, supplemented with corn meal mush with bacon grease in it. They had, for a better name, running fits. This caused them to foam at the mouth, run in circles, and seek a dark place usually under the house, some people were afraid of them in this condition but they were harmless and soon recovered.

We know now, that these so called fits were caused by a protein deficiency in their almost total diet of corn meal mush. We never would have figured this out because we ate the same thing that they did and we didn't have running fits. At least most didn't.

I was glad to know that the fame of hot water corn bread lives on, when Norma Dell Jones asked for a recipe in one of her articles. I was glad to pass one a little different on to her. I have had several experiences with young people and hot water corn bread. I served it to a bunch on a deer camp many years ago and they thought it was the greatest thing since Ivory soap. One man had his cook call me for the recipe. When I told her what it was her reply was, why Mr. Bob that ain't nothing but dog bread. I told her not to tell him just lay it on him every time she cooked turnip greens.

I used to enjoy fixing a big bunch of turnip or collard greens, baked sweet potatoes, fresh pork with gravy, fresh green onions, if available, if not onions pickled in vinegar, radishes, and hot water corn bread. Dessert would be hot bread with ribbon cane syrup. Our friends really enjoyed it. Now you can't afford to go to the trouble because it seems just about everybody is on a diet. The next worse thing is to invite some one to supper and they ask you what the menu is. The worst thing is to have them come and tell you that their diet doesn't include what you have fixed.

My latest experience with this wonderful dish was last week on a bird hunt in North Texas. I fixed my usual meal of mustard and turnip greens, baked sweet potato, fresh hog meat from a hog trapped on the Sullivan ranch, fresh onions, and hot water corn bread. It drew the usual response even for the ones who forgot their diet and loaded up on everything. There was one thing that I had not seen since childhood and that was one young man who poured syrup on his turnip greens. That let me know that all was not lost from the old days and that some of this younger generation have more appreciation of good food than I have given them credit for.

MAD DOGS

In my last article about the delights of corn bread, I touched on the subject of dots and running fits. As I stated then, the dogs were harmless in this condition but they scared the bejabbers out of some who thought they might be rabid. Rabies was common back when I was a kid because most people didn't vaccinate their pets. But there was a big difference in running fits and rabies.

Rabies or hydrophobia (fear of water) was more prevalent in dogs and cats back then because they came in contact with infected animals more often and were bitten. People back then, especially out in the country, were always on the lookout for wild animals that showed no fear of humans and were acting strangely. If one of these animals were suspected of biting a dog or cat, the dog or cat was locked up and observed for a week or so.

My first experience with rabies and mad dogs happened when I was about ten years old. I had brought a little small stray female collie dog home with me telling my Mother that I had done my best to run it off, when I had really fed it candy to get it to follow me home.

She had a litter of puppies, I believe about five of them, and before they were weaned she disappeared. I had noticed that she didn't act quite right and she looked like she was going blind. I didn't think anything about it. I spread the puppies around keeping one and giving one to our back door neighbor.

Some time later on a freezing morning I heard a scratching at our door and there was the neighbor's puppy. I let it in and as I was sitting down the puppy bit me in the thigh with the force of a full grown dog. I knew right away that the puppy was mad and I told my sister to get on a chair. I had to use all my strength to pry the puppy loose from my leg and when I got loose it latched onto my thumb and I had trouble getting loose again. The puppy was put outside and later locked up where it was destroyed and its head sent to Austin.

Of course the results were positive and I, my sister, and half the kids in town had to take the rabies shots when the doctor finally received them. The treatment then was a shot a day for twenty one days. They were rather painful having to be given with a big needle in the lower part of the stomach and when that space was used up, you were jabbed in the behind.

I have often thought that it was rather strange that the mother dog bit her puppies but never made any effort to bite any of us kids. Maybe it was because of her affection for me that prevented her from hurting me. I will always wonder.

My maternal grandmother used to tell the story of one of our ancestors who had rabies and was confined to bed. She said his attacks came in waves and when he felt one coming on he had them tie him to the bed until it passed. Of course there is no treatment for rabies after it starts.

Maybe my dog knew when she was in the biting stage and left so she wouldn't bite me. In looking back that puppy that bit me might have saved many lives because we might have already been infected by playing with the little female or one of her puppies and not have been aware of it.

Being rather a slow learner, I have had the rabies shots again having been bitten by a rabid fox. We were on a training exercise in North Carolina during the war and were camped out in the freezing cold. Now the Army training back then consisted in teaching you how to starve to death for water and how to freeze to death in cold weather.

We had a two man tent called a pup tent consisting of three closed sides and one open side. The practice then was for four men to put two tents together and be completely closed in. During such an arrangement early on a freezing morning an animal tried to get into our tent. As luck would have it he was working just above my head and as I tried to knock it off it bit through the canvas and got my finger. It was a fox and one was killed later that had rabies. That later treatment was only fifteen shots still with a horse needle and in the stomach.

I remember those shots quite well and who gave them. Six of us had been in a car wreck a short time before, with none of us seriously injured, and we had a big time while we were in the hospital causing the nurses, especially a big old homely one, a lot of trouble.

I knew I was in trouble when I walked in for my first shot and the homely nurse greeted me with the statement, "fox bites wolf." I will always believe that she used an extra long needle on me to pay me back for the trouble that we had caused her. So much for Mad dogs and homely nurses.

What's in a Name

It has long been said that the sweetest sound to a person is the sound of their own name. This is true for most of us I suppose, and especially for politicians. What brought this to mind was the naming contests that were conducted during the early days of the Houston County Development Foundation. The naming of the Foundation its self was never in doubt because it served the whole County. The Airport was bought with money raised by the people and given to the County. Now the County was like Leroy, who didn't want the ball, and didn't really want the responsibility of building and maintaining an airport but eventually took hold and the airport was named for the County. Our wonderful library was named for Dr. John H. Wooters who contributed so much to its existence, The Porth Arena for the Porth family who owned the land and so on down the line.

Many naming contest took place down through the years but the big one was the naming of our new lake on Little Elkhart Creek. As I remember a $50.00 dollar prize was offered for the name chosen. This caused quite a bit of excitement in the County, not only for the honor of having your name chosen, but back then a fifty dollar bill was as big as a saddle blanket and not to be sneezed at. Many clever names were submitted including such as Tejas Shores Lake, Big Springs Lake, Eagles Rest Lake, Little Elkhart Lake, Green Shores Lake, and so on. Finally the Committee after deliberating for many hours and keeping the whole County in suspense, reached a decision and named it Houston County Lake. Now that took some doing.

After many more contest were held finally another big one came up. This involved naming a new bakery and sandwich shop that had opened in Crockett. A wonderful lady, named Bernice Brimberry, who formally operated a grocery store in Grapeland moved to Crockett and opened a grocery store and bakery shop. She was very active in everything of a Civic nature and also served on the City Council. Every one knew and admired her. She decided to hold a naming contest for her new business on South Fourth Street and she would be the judge. I think she also offered a $50.00 Prize.

There was much talk about this contest especially among the school children. Like the Lake contest, many unique and clever names were submitted. Some that I remember were, Hole In One, Eat and Dunk, Dunk and Go, Burger and Sweets, The In and Out, Why Not? Bernice's Burgers, and so on.

Finally and after much deliberation. Bernice selected the winner who was a young school girl and today a grandmother here in Crockett who remembered about the sound of a persons name and wisely submitted the winning name of "Brimberry's Bakery and Grill, thus proving that the old name thing adage still lives.

Playing Football

I saw in the paper that the Crockett High School had lined up their coaching personnel for the coming school year. It involved twelve men and eight women making a total of twenty people to see that we have a strong athletic program.

It sure is different from my football playing days. When I was a freshman in high school my family moved from a football crazy town to one where most people knew very little about the game.

This was in 1935, and I played on the first football team that the school ever had. It was something to behold. I was the only member who had ever touched a football and just one other player had ever even seen a football game.

We had to buy our shoes and athletic supporters and we had to bring our game day jerseys home to be washed. Remember this was in the midst of the depression in the days of five cent hamburgers, ten cent gasoline, and one dollar a day wages.

We had about fourteen boys come out for practice in old uniforms that our coach had salvaged from his old school. The biggest man on the squad weighed less than one hundred seventy pounds. I checked in at five foot nine and one hundred thirty five pounds.

I guess we were a 2A school and most of our opponents were schools in the heart of the East Texas Oil Field and had the finest equipment and players that money could buy. They killed us.

The rules were much different back then. You didn't have players running on and off the field. If you left the game in one quarter you could not come back in the game until the next quarter. The coach could only come on the field if you were injured and then he couldn't talk about the game, only about the injury.

The quarters were twelve minutes as they are today and with only twelve to fourteen men suited up, we became forty eight minute players. During the time out between quarters the water boy came out with the water bucket. I mean a tin bucket with a dipper. At the end of each quarter, and the three time outs, plus the half time intermission, was the only time you got a drink. What made it tougher was that all games were afternoon games.

Our home games were played on a cow pasture behind the school where the cows had been run off and two by four goal posts erected and lines were laid off with lime. The fresh cow patties were scooped up and carried to the side line but nothing was done about the grass burrs. We spent our time outs picking grass burrs out of our jerseys.

We did not have a high school band but we did have a pep squad, which did their best to find something to cheer about. The people from the little town really took to football and sometimes there would be fifteen or twenty fans on the sidelines. No bleachers back then .

My career ended at the end of my senior year when I broke my nose. I knew it was broken, my parents knew it was broken but the old doctor that they took me to in the back of the drug store who was busy writing prescriptions for whiskey stopped long enough to wiggle my nose a few times and said he thought it would be okay. It was not okay then and has not been since. Since we had no such things as face guards back then to protect my broken nose, that ended my playing days.

We established a school record that has stood until this day. We won one game in three years. I really believe that we would have done better if we could have had twelve coaches back then.

I hope that there is enough money left from hiring all those coaches to hire some additional teachers to teach the kids how to read and write and make a living when they finish school. We can only hope.

What a Shame

As I observe the mess that our City Government has sunk into, I feel not only ashamed but guilty. Ashamed that others know about the debacle going on and a feeling of guilt because maybe I could have done something, or at least tried, to prevent it from taking place.

When I think o the great leaders, both Black and White, who worked so hard to make this town a better place to work and live, I know they must be weeping with sorrow over what has happened.

Leaders who worked for better schools where ignorant people could send their children to prepare them for a productive life. These leaders worked hard and paid taxes so these children could enjoy a good home, free food, free medical and dental care, and other necessities of life.

These same leaders worked to get jobs for the people, for hospitals, libraries, nursing homes, an airport, good drinking water, better utilities, better streets, better race relations, and many other things that people today take for granted.

This great Country of ours was built on good sense. The good sense to try and choose our best to represent us beginning with George Washington, then Lincoln, and so on down to the present. Sometimes a bad apple got in but that was a mistake and was soon corrected. The age old custom of selecting our best to serve us has stood the test of time and is alive today.

Even today with all the information that radio, television, and newspapers have to offer, we still get fooled and elect the wrong people to office. If we let someone fool us once shame on them, if we let them do it again, shame on us.

May God bless America and this town. This may be the only solution.

ALARM SYSTEMS

The other day I was coming out of the Methodist Church and I heard the wootle-wootle of what we call a "Booger Alarm" some where beyond the Baptist Church and when I came back that night I still heard it, or another one, that was going full blast. I thought it was unusual because in my experience they usually only go off at night when no one is home.

I have had quite a bit of experience with those things, not my own because I don't have one, but with neighbors and friends systems. We keep a key to several of their houses in order to kind of look after things for them when they are not home.

I could write a small book about the alarm systems that I have come in contact with. I have made several trips across the street to turn off one system, never knowing what had tripped the thing. Same thing with the Boy's and Girl's Club out at the Park. It is all the time going off for no obvious reason, and I know our fine police officers, as well as myself, are getting tired of answering those false alarms.

Before we got a key to his house, one neighbors system went off when they were out of town and wootled for hours before being turned off. Another time these same neighbors went out of town and left their cat in the house. When the police officer and I unlocked the door a day or two later that cat climbed all over us getting out of there.

Then there was the time when the alarm company called me in the middle of the night that the alarm in a friends house at the Spring Creek Country Club was going off. The house was about quarter mile beyond a locked gate and when I got there, an officer's car had it blocked and I had to walk in. As usual we saw no sign of break in and the only thing missing was some sleep.

The one I remember the most was one that would have been a good episode for a Keystone Cops movie. Our back door friends were out of town and he called me to get something from his house and bring to the deer lease. He had shown me the alarm system control box and how it worked, but that had been a long time ago and of course I didn't pay much attention to the details.

I went over to the house late that afternoon unlocked the door and as I was looking for the control box the thing went off. I finally got it shut off found the item he wanted, reset the controls, locked the house, and went home.

About midnight the thing went off again. The police and I arrived at the same time and with guns drawn they pushed me aside and went storming through the house. After a complete check of the premises the culprit was found. It was their little dog that I had accidentally let in on my previous visit. He had tripped a censor and set the thing off. The police left, I put dog out, reset the system locked the house, and went back to bed.

About two thirty in the morning I heard the dreaded sound of "wootle-wootle, and I knew where it was coming from. I got my flashlight and my pistol and here I went even though I knew that it was surely another false alarm I felt somewhat apprehensive going into that dark house at that time of night. But go in I did, cut off the cursed thing and started looking. It didn't take long to find the cause; a loose door that the officers hadn't completely closed. This time I made sure that I did not reset the machine, locked the door, and finally back to bed.

Of course back in my young days we didn't have such a contraption to warn us of trespassers, we had dogs at night and guinea's during the day. A flock of guinea's could spot someone coming long before a dog ever thought about it. Also their constant chatter was a soothing sound to a lonely farm wife.

In Medieval times peacocks were used as look outs on top castles as they could spot some one approaching from a great distance away. Guinea's would have probably done them a better job as lookouts and we know that you can't beat guinea eggs for breakfast or anytime for that matter.

Good Cooks & Others

In some of my past ramblings I have made reference to my cooking. I am by my own admission a pretty good Country Cook. I have been asked how long that I have been at it. I started by helping my Mother get a meal on the table when I was in a hurry to eat and get gone.

My Mother was a very good cook but sometimes was a little slow in getting everything ready at the same time, a situation that I have become very familiar with after fifty six years of marriage. Having to use a wood burning stove and toting water from a well had something to do with it. I would help her finish a dish and gradually began to learn how to do several dishes.

We kids used to do what we called "sleeping out" that included cooking a stew. Each one would bring something from the house to throw in the pot. I got tired of eating scorched stew so I began doing it myself. Back then, we didn't get to run to the store for candy when we wanted it, so my Mother taught me how to make chocolate fudge candy. I still remember how today. Take cocoa, sugar, milk, butter, vanilla extract, and some karo syrup and if you took it up at the right time, and beat it long enough, you had a creamy creation that was hard to beat. My Grandmother used to add peanut butter to hers.

This experience came in handy later on in our hunting camps. In order to cut down on waste, I bought all the groceries myself. I learned never to let a bunch of hunters go shopping with me because they picked up everything they saw, most of which was never used. I tried to never have much food left to throw out when we broke camp.

I have had many wives tell me that their husbands were good cooks. When I ask them what they cooked, they almost all say they can broil a good steak. I never learned to broil a steak in my younger days, mainly because we didn't have that kind of meat. Also back then, I don't recall ever seeing a man in the kitchen unless he was just passing through, much less cooking. It was a woman's domain and she usually ruled it. My daddy never made any attempt to cook. In fact he never even got up for a glass of water if someone was there to get it for him.

Sometimes when someone would catch a mess of fish the men would fire up an old wash pot full of hog lard and fry the fish but the women would fix everything else. Same thing with oysters when someone would bring a bucket of them packed in ice from town. We kids could never under stand how some of the men could eat them raw.

My definition of a good cook, is a man who is told when he comes home that there is not a thing to eat in the house, and a while later he comes up with a meal for six or eight people sitting it on the table using only stuff from the freezer and the pantry.

Also a good cook is someone who don't use any ingredient that he can't spell or that cannot be found in the local stores. Good cooking takes imagination and daring to try something new. Take hush puppies for instance. The simplest and most common ingredients are the hardest to make to come out right. I fattened many a bird dog with my failures.

I hear many people my age wishing for the good old days of home grown vegetables, home cured meat, home made pies, hot cornbread and biscuits, jersey cow milk, and many more childhood dishes. I look back with nostalgia on some of those memories but we can be thankful for some of the modern customs.

One thing that had been completely reversed is the practice back then of cooking inside and going to the toilet outside. I think any one in their right mind is thankful for this change.

THE SWIMMING POOL

Every once in a while something will come up that will remind me of an event that took place long ago. Such was the case the other day when Hester Faye Bobbitt, who lost her husband Merle awhile back, brought me an old picture showing Merle and me standing beside this bull dozier, with Roger Benton at the controls, moving the first dirt for the construction of the swimming pool.

It brought back a flood of memories. Memories of a group of young men and women who returned home for the war and decided to change things. The vehicles for this change were the Jaycees for the men and the Beta Sigma Phi for the women. Many things were done but the first and greatest project was to build a swimming pool.

You must remember back then there were no big lakes such as we have today. Outside of a creek, a stock tank, or the river, about the only place left to learn to swim was the Spring Creek Country Club Lake and access to this was limited by membership requirements.

So with the naiveté of youth we jumped into the project of building a swimming pool. The first hurdle was to get the land. It was to be a private association and segregated, so City Park land could not be used. The spot chosen was a tract just west of the old K.I.V.Y. radio station. The man who owned this land was noted for his frugality. He was very consistent in his giving never giving to anything.

We choose a group of our most smooth talking Jaycees to go talk him out of some land. They took the American flag, a Bible, and several more items that might help influence him. All their efforts netted them one half acre of land. Now this same group said this was a snap compared to their second trip to get an additional one tenth acre of land from him.

We had to have someone to design the thing and supervise the project. We were very fortunate in finding a local man who was well qualified and would donate his time. That man was Staley Mims who was a Col., in the Corps of Engineers during the WWII and who had designed and was in charge of the new sewer system being constructed at that time.

Now it was the time to move dirt and this is when Merle Bobbitt, and many others donated their equipment and their efforts for this project. There were many more that I may have overlooked that did all they could to help. Remember this was during one of the worst droughts on record and the post oak ground was like concrete. You could almost see sparks fly when the dozier blades dug in. The Machines could only go so far and it had to be finished by shovel and wheel barrow. The dirt on the sides had to be pried off in chunks using a sharp tool. I still have the old Model "T" axle that George Young, Sr. made into a tool for me.

All this time money was being raised and materials donated to complete the project. People opened their hearts and their pocket books to an extent never seen before or since.

We were fortunate that a new process for applying concrete had been perfected using a method of spraying the concrete directly on the dirt which eliminated the need for wooden forms. There was no new technology for unloading a boxcar load of concrete which had to be done by hand.

Most of the work was done at night because most of us worked at a job during the day. Our wives, many who were Beta Sigma Phi's, would bring us our supper and we labored under the bright lights way into the night, night after night.

Finally it was finished and the valves were opened to fill the pool and the wading pool that the Beta Sigma Phi's had built. On opening day there was to be a big celebration with a diving team from the University of Texas, speeches, and many more things.

The night before the grand opening, some of us were doing last minute things and watching the pool fill. We thought it only fitting that we be the first ones to take a dip in our pool. Since we had no bathing suits and no one was watching we decided to shuck off our clothes and dive in. Now let the record show that there were no Beta Sigma Phi's in this caper, only Jaycees. It would probably have been more memorable the other way.

The pool passed into history due to changing times, apathy, and short sightedness on the part of the City Government at that time. It is now owned by the Boy's and Girl's Club.

To borrow a phrase from Winston Churchill "It was our finest hour." If you were to ask Mutt Knox, Jake Caprielian, John McCall,Sr., Dan Julian, Sr. Jim Gibbs, Grady Lake, Vaughn Reyen, Carl Murray, or W. H. Holcomb, what they remember most about building the pool, chances are they will say "unloading the concrete" which would be my answer.

EULOGIES

Eulogies, whose history goes back to recorded time did not come into general use at funerals in East Texas until after WWII, at least not in the Protestant churches that are prevalent in our area.

Any eulogies of the sort were usually delivered by the unfortunate minister who must do his utmost to get the deceased, who in many cases had lived a life of sin, up the Pearly Gates to be judged.

It is a tough job for a minister and especially for a laymen to deliver a eulogy. In some cases it requires stretching the truth to its breaking point to emphasize the high points of the deceased life while skillfully brushing over his low points. To clear his conscience the deliverer can always remember his words are not for the departed but for the survivors who face him.

The one to give the eulogy is usually a friend of the deceased who had known him for many years, and one that the family had asked to do this. It is a great honor to be asked to do this but in my case it was one of the hardest things that I have ever attempted.

I was fortunate in the ones that I have been asked to do because I had known each of the men since WWII and knew both their dark sides as well as their light sides. By emphasizing their light side injected with bits of humor would usually help to relax the tension a bit and replace some tears with a smile.

You certainly brought out all the good points that the minister might have over looked but overall you stuck with the lighter side. If you could reduce the sadness and gloom of the service and leave a bit of a happy feeling then you felt better for having done it.

I have always thought the purpose of the minister and the Church service was to get the deceased up to the Pearly Gates, and the purpose of the eulogy was to present his light side to a Judge you hoped had a sense of humor.

Eulogy To Willie Hayne Knox

I could visualize this scene before I came into this sanctuary today. I knew that you, in attendance, would represent friends from every walk of life. Not only the friends of the one we came to pay our last respects to but friends of his family as well.

We gather today to pay our final respects to Willie "Baby Hayne" Knox. A man who spent his lifetime doing it "his way," and I might add, in most cases, getting away with it. His slogan was "whatever's right."

I stepped off a bus in Crockett in February, 1946 fresh from duty in WWII. I did not know anyone. The first person I met was Nat Patton, Jr. Later on I met Delbert Knox, Willie's uncle who was kind enough to introduce me to the Knox family. Willie and I knocked around in the fast lane a couple years while I dated his sister Peggy.

In early 1948 Peggy and I agreed that under the circumstances it would be best to go our separate ways. Willie got wind of this and one night used some excuse to get me into his car where we went straight to his daddy's house and went in. We ran into Peggy and Willie said "Miss Knox, I would like for you to meet Mr. Mattox." With that said he turned and left. Things progressed from that night to our wedding in June. I shall ever be indebted to him for his actions that night.

The day of the wedding Peggy was all nervous and broken out in a wedding day rash. Here came Willie popping his chewing gum as only he could. He said "Peggy, if you have changed your mind about marrying that s.o.b. here is some money and there's a brand new car in the driveway with the motor running."

I guess you could describe him as a combination of Pecks bad boy and Huckleberry Finn. What ever he did, and he did his share, instead of people censoring they would laugh and say "that Baby Hayne is a card." Every one liked him and he liked everybody. People wanted to do things for him without his asking it.

I have heard Peggy tell how his sisters used to help him get ready for a date. One would lay out his clothes, one would shine his shoes, and one would go pick up his date. He was always dressed fit to kill usually with Mutt's last clean shirt on.

This habit of someone looking after him extended to our deer hunts. Many a time he hit camp with only his street clothes on. The next morning when hunt time came he would be out fitted in warm long johns, hunting pants, a warm shirt, cap, gloves, jacket, field glasses, deer rifle, flashlight, and a cushion to sit on always in someone else's stand. There was no big thing about this as it happened every year just like the sun rising in the East.

He was the most uncomplicated person that I've ever known. He dealt with the moment at hand in a simple direct manner and when that moment was over it was gone and forgotten.

I recall one morning either on a hunting or fishing trip when he got up before I did and said "Brother-in-law, I forgot my tooth brush and I used yours." To him that was a simple solution to a simple problem. There is no doubt that had the circumstances been reversed I would have been welcome to his. He was the only person I ever knew who could walk down a street in Mexico, eating out of every vendors cart and not be bothered at all.

I have never known him to hold a grudge. I have known of some pretty serious run-ins that he had with people, some in this audience, but when it was over, it was water under the bridge and the fact that he could put these things behind him made it easier for the other party to do the same. I have always admired him for this trait.

He loved his family and his home. His home and yard, his business premises, and Knox cabin were always kept neat and clean. During his tenure as president of the

Country Club, by using his own equipment and money, and against opposition I might added, made much needed improvements to the Club.

He made great sacrifices to see that his children got all the education that they would take advantage of and to hold his family together during some trying times.

The tradition of everyone reaching out to help him extended to his last days when the Mother of his children came back to help take care of him. He did not consider this unusual at all. He accepted this with gratitude although he had difficulty expressing it.

My Boy, if you are aware of your many friends presence here today and the many expressions of sympathy and acts of kindness rendered to your family, knowing you, I can almost hear you "Now ain't this something." And in truth, it is.

Eulogy To Harold Mack (Red Bull) Walker

We are assembled here today to say farewell to Harold Mack (Red Bull) Walker one of Crockett's better known characters and I might venture to say from the response here today one of Crockett's beloved characters.

He was raised by his grandparents on a hard scrabble farm in North Texas during the depression when like everyone else, he had to make out with the barest necessities and a simple gift at Xmas was a rare treat. He never forgot this.

At an early age he joined the Marines and worked himself up through the ranks to become an officer. He met Mary and they got married in Japan. Compared to their nuptials we here are just kinda married. They had three different ceremonies.

He finished his education and started a successful career. All this time he never forgot his childhood and the gifts that he never received and he made sure that his children and those around him would have a reason to celebrate Christmas.

Christmas at the Walker house was something to remember. There would be gifts piled under the tree that would make Macey's and Toys-R-Us envious. After the traditional Christmas breakfast of salmon patties was finished, the gifts were opened and by the time this was finished, the wrappings would be almost hip deep in the big room. All this time Mary would be looking through the big house for the gifts that she had been hiding all year. That afternoon the whole Walker bunch, plus whoever else wanted to go, would head for Red River.

Red River. None of us who had the privilege of being their guest there will ever forget it. The routine never varied. When we arrived Mary and Harold had forgotten to bring their keys and we had to break in the cabin. I am not talking about an isolated incident I am talking about almost every time we went. It became a joke that if you went with the Walkers to Red River you took some tools to break in with. This never bothered Harold one bit.

The Walkers have always been noted for their hospitality. Many don't know that they had the first Bed and Breakfast establishment in Crockett. Not only bed and breakfast, but lunch, and supper, bed again, breakfast, and so on sometimes lasting for months. Their house was a refuge for family and others going through difficult times. This was done through the goodness of their hearts. As many times as I have been in their beautiful home I have never figured out where everyone sleeps. The guest and family would disappear at night and show up in the morning.

Harold never met a stranger. When he met someone they became his friend. Harold's hospitality extended to the strangers whose car broke down in front of his house. They stayed with the Walkers while their car was being repaired. Then there was the Japanese girl who came to visit on the Lions Club Student Exchange program who extended her visit to finish Crockett High School and enter college before her father came over to take her home.

He never forgot his Marine Corps buddies, and when ever we happened to pass through a town where one lived, we always stopped where Harold not only offered a word of encouragement but in many cases left a check.

He loved to play golf and to be charitable, we will call him a fair golfer. He always had trouble getting off the tee box, but when he got around the green he would kill you. A few Sunday's ago during our Sunday School lesson, reference was made to a silent prayer that golfers say hoping their shot would be down the middle. Harold said his prayer was that he could find his ball after he hit it. This was brought home to us when we played a round of golf on a mountainous course in Japan. We set a course record when we lost twenty one balls. He never gave up on a hole no matter how many strokes it took. This determined streak contributed to his success in the business world.

Walker son if your entreaties down through the years to the "Great Architect of the Universe have been acknowledged your golf swing by now has been corrected, and you have been reunited with Jim Tom, Reed, Bubba, Henry, Willie Hayne, plus many other friends." Chances are by now you and Willie have already made your Super Bowl bets and gotten up a game of dominoes. From the depths of our hearts we hope this is so.

Eulogy To Grady Lake
March 14, 2006

We are gathered here today to bid fare well and Godspeed to Grady (Bubba) Lake, one of Crockett's fast disappearing colorful characters who always did it his way.

He was born during the depression, finished high school where he was a very popular student who played in the band and also played football. He served four and one half years in the Navy in WWII. He graduated from North Texas State where he met Joann.

Always a hustler from early age and while in college he delivered papers, and sold Fuller brushes. Jake Caprielian recalls an incident when he went to North Texas, to visit

Jill and dropped in on Grady and Joann and left with an arm load of brushes that he didn't need.

I first met Grady in 1951 when I finished A & M and opened a service station here in Crockett. Grady and Billy McLean both college graduates, had just opened a station along with a college graduate named Tucker who opened one causing an old time station owner to complain that you had to be a college graduate to open a service station in Crockett.

He tried house building, truck farming, raising, chickens, hauling chickens, operating a corn sheller, boat business, hunting preserve, Dude Ranch, you name it he would try it. Seeing him through all this was his unfailing sense of wit and humor.

All of his living friends with whom I have talked had an anecdote to relate about Grady and his sense of humor. One I remember from way back was when we were admiring his first house he built and his reply was: "Thank you, I wish that I could afford it."

Another that brought down the house was at a wedding rehearsal that we were both in and the bossy wedding director was ready for the best man and asked Grady if he was the best man and he said: "yes ma'm I really am but the bride doesn't know it."

One that struck with Dr. John McCall was when a man was trying to sell Grady a real good bird dog for $500.00 and Grady asked him if he would trade for two $250.00 cats.

Grady was also a smooth talker and could charm almost anyone into doing something at least once anyway. This was demonstrated one night when we stuck our one vehicle on the banks of the Trinity River on the McCall place and had to walk out. We finally came to a house about halfway to Grapeland that had a pulp wood truck parked in the yard. We roused the man of the house and out came a Marcell Ledbetter type out the door with just his overalls on with one strap buckled and he was big. Grady talked him into taking us to Grapeland and once we got there, he talked him into taking us on to Crockett and once there, we discovered that none of us had any money, Grady talked him into taking a check. Probably who ever wrote the check had to beat it to the bank because none of us had any money back then.

Grady's sense of humor caused him to employ colorful characters and one that I remember was called "Foot." Now Foot, a slow thinking black man, was aptly named because the largest shoe available was a little tight on his foot.

Other incidents come to mind, one when Grady came to the rescue of a small friend of his who was being beaten by a much larger man. Grady not only pulled the big man off but also gave him a pretty good going over in the process.

Another incident that John McCall remembers was the time that he and Elvira were visiting Grady and Joann when they were living in the upstairs garage apartment behind Dr. Lakes house. Their young daughter Pam who was just learning to crawl, was about to crawl off the porch on to some jagged rocks below when Grady caught and prevented what could have been a very serious injury.

Back during his early years when he was struggling to provide for his family, work with the Jaycees, and take care of his many other projects, before the days of boats, airplanes, hunting lodges, and his later pleasures, his main hobby was quail hunting. That was back when we had quail in Houston and neighboring Counties. We all had good dogs and hunted together.

We took real good care of our dogs with all the shots, flea control, and good dog food that we thought that they required, while Grady's dogs in most case's were free to roam the farm taking care of themselves the best they could, and come hunting season his dogs would find just as many, and sometimes more birds than our dogs.

Grady was a "jack of all trades" and master of some but not all. He would try anything and if that failed jump right into something else. This lasted to the last when during the last year of his life he built a shed next to the house doing most of the work himself.

Grady and Joann suffered the tragedy of losing a son. They like others before and since had to find their own way to cope with this. Some will say that a tragedy like this is God's will and that's pretty hard to accept. A few would say it is God's punishment, and this is unacceptable because if you accept this it will not only ruin you life, but the lives of those around you. Grady and Joann accepted this as something that just happened and that there is no answer for this on this earth, but to go on with their lives.

As we sit here today based on the strength of our faith in God, we must believe that a merciful Creator has removed your pain and you are in a place full of quail. Chances are you have traded your two cats for a good bird dog and can hunt to your hearts content.

From the bottoms of our hearts we hope this is so.

Eulogy To Jim Dubcak

This brief Jim Dubcak eulogy was requested by his wife Helen and was published in the June 2002 issue of "The Young At Heart Herald."

He wasn't a big man in statue, but big in heart.
He seldom spoke in a loud voice (especially around Helen)
But when he spoke he usually had something to say.
He was blessed in being financially secure,
Yet had empathy for those less fortunate.
His life was his Helen and His Church.
He will be missed.

WWII & Seabiscuit

When my boy's were young and would ask me what I did during World War II, I would tell them about the Great Depression, and joining the army as an escape from a dead end job, also about seeing much of this great Country. Riding in gliders, jumping out of airplanes, a troop ship ride to France, plus many other adventures, and it use to pass completely over their heads. If it happened today and I told them that at one time I got to pet the race horse called, Seabiscuit, that would have probably stuck.

As I mentioned before, in 1940 in order to make a change, I joined a National Guard Unit. We were part of the 36th Division and were sent to Camp Bowie in Brownwood, Texas. Being among the first arrivals we stayed in tents and slogged through the black mud that passed for streets.

If any of remember the opening movie scene when Patton told the troops that when their children asked them what they did during the War that they wouldn't have to say that they spent the war shoveling manure in Louisiana. I did that. We spent three weeks in the summer of 1941 sleeping in tents, marching in 100 degree heat and all this time trying to learn how to do with little food and water, "I will say this," we got tough.

There are many dates that people never forget such as the Kennedy assignation, 911, the birth of a baby, and so on, but there is one date that is burned into my memory and that is December 7, 1941 when we learned that Pearl Harbor had been bombed. We knew then, playing war games was over and we had been placed in harms way.

Within ten days we were loaded into a Troop Train and headed for the West coast. That's when a new world opened up for a group of East Texas country boys, who had never eaten a shrimp cocktail, or knew what a mixed drink was, and most having never been more than a few miles from home. Some came from farther back in the country than others. In fact we had one old boy we called "Git Wood." He claimed that he didn't know what his real name was until he joined the Army.

To get back to my story, we were on the train for five days because we had to side track to let the other trains pass. During one such side tract in Northern California is when we saw a horse in a paddock next to the rail road track. Some one said it was the race horse called Seabiscuit. What ever horse it was, I got to pet it.

Another incident that I remember is on another stop some of our boys jumped five deer and killed three of them and brought them onto the train. What was so memorable was those were the first wild deer that any of us had ever seen. Back when we were kids there were no deer left in East Texas, because they had all been killed for food during the depression. There were few squirrels, coons, rabbits, possums, or other small game all having met the same fate as the deer. One thing that we did have in abundance was bob white quail. Poor people didn't hunt them because there was no way that they would spend a nickel or a shell to try to kill a six ounce bird when that shell might be used to kill a squirrel or a rabbit.

From the west Coast, I went to Officer Training School, was assigned to an Airborne unit, rode in gliders, jumped out of planes, rode a Troop ship, saw Europe, and after more than five years in the Service, came to Crockett, finished my education, married, had children, and managed to put some back for our old age. Strangely, after sixty three years, what I still remember most vividly is not petting the horse, but the boys killing the deer.

Diets Versus Common Sense

Time was when you set down at a table laden with what was then conceived as healthy food, and gave thanks to the Creator for providing it. There was no concern as to calories or proteins mainly because most cooks wouldn't have known what you were talking about. The main concern being that everybody left the table full of food that stuck to their ribs and would last them until the next meal.

What a contrast today. As a result of our sedentary life style we have a society of people who are obsessed with trying to lose weight and in their zeal to find the magic solution, they have embraced every diet fad that has come forward. Instead of being thankful for a bountiful table full of good food they feel guilty when eating it.

Here's one that says no bread, rice, potatoes, no fruit, but plenty of meat, eggs, and cheese. This guru recently died of heart failure due to clogged arteries. But wait, here's one that says a diet including meat is bad for your health.

Let's shop around and find something that might suit you. Here is a conclusion by a group of doctors that says meat, milk and eggs may not be healthy for your heart. Don't suit you? The American Dietetic Association say bread, vegetables, fruits, milk, and meat are permissible. Getting closer?

Want to try a high protein one? As we move along here is a study that concludes that a high protein diet may cause kidney stones. Another study says too much protein in the blood stream can cause heart disease.

We learn that too much salt, which would be no more that you put on your egg in the morning is too much and may cause high blood pressure. But wait, chocolate may lower blood pressure. Hooray for Hershey bars, especially with almonds, nuts are okay you know.

As we fill our children with orange juice each morning to ward off the build up of cholesterol we learn that too much builds up potassium which can cause kidney stones. As we stuff ourselves with vitamins each day, we want to be careful that we do not build up too much iron in the blood stream because it may cause diabetes.

Suffer leg cramps? Lack of potassium. Need 4700 milligrams a day. Eat bananas. How many? A bunch of them, or drink a jug of orange juice a day. Leg cramps or maybe kidney stones? Looks like you just can't win.

Drinking lots of water, up to eight big glasses a day, was recommended, which is a gallon of water. They now say drink only what you want. One obvious advantage to this is that it should cut down trips to the bathroom, especially at night.

You have probably noticed that each so-called diet recommendation has the disclaimer "may" in front of it and states that it has worked on mice. It is comforting to know that we have a population of healthy mice. Now we see that they think dogs will do better than mice to experiment with. What happened to guinea pigs?

We are a nation of over weight people with many who are severely obese. We have the disease prevalent in Africa, called the Nodding Disease whereby people afflicted with this malady start nodding when they see food and then fall to the floor. We have fat people in this Country with the same symptoms who began nodding when they are asked if they want a second helping and keep nodding for more.

In our ceaseless effort to find a simple way to eat what's good and keep off weight we have abandoned common sense and embraced every fad diet that has come out, including some that have proved to be harmful. In the process, we have made some smart people rich while we get fatter. There are some simple diet plans. One that I remember is the "Push Back Plan" whereby you push your chair back from the table before you get full. One plan that is catching on fast is one that originated here in Crockett and is spreading all over the Country. It cost nothing, is simple, and is guaranteed to work. It is called "The Poor Man's Diet Plan" or "If It Taste Good Spit It Our Diet Plan." You might try this one.

EGRETS HAVE COME TO TOWN

I have heard several people say that they have been seeing a large white bird in their backyards lately. Although, the African Cattle Egret has been in Houston County ever since I have been here, this is the first time that I have ever seen one in town. Supposedly they were blown into the U.S. by a hurricane.

Time was when there were few, if any crows in town. They have come to town because their natural food source is gradually being destroyed. The oak, hickory, the native pecan trees, the chinquapin, huckleberry, black haw, wild grapes vines, muskidimes, mayhaws, and many other things that not only were eaten by crows but also by people, are gone with the times.

During my lifetime, many species have moved from West to East. Just lately I have seen grackles here in Crockett. These black birds look like a cross between a crow and our black bird. Their tail feathers run up and down instead of flat like other birds. They make a terrible racket and mess.

I was raised in North East Texas, and I never saw a jack rabbit, an armadillo, a coyote, a rattlesnake, deer, or a fire ant until I came to Crockett right after WWII. When I was ranching, I had quit a bit of exposure to the coyote and found them to be a most interesting animal. Some ranchers claim to have had calves killed by them, but if

I did, I never knew it. They would follow a new born calf to eat the rich droppings but I never saw them harm one. The cows would pay no more attention to than they would a dog that came across the pasture.

We had quite a few coyotes on the Leo Knox ranch just South of town, mainly because of the dead chickens from the chicken farm up the road. We also had to dispose of many dead calves from our yearling program at the ranch. I often wondered why we didn't see many buzzards, like we used to when something died. The mystery was solved one day when a calf died almost while I was watching. A few buzzards started circling. About this time I saw coyotes coming at a dead run from every direction. That ended the buzzard circling. It was at least a week before the coyotes finished and let the buzzards take over. That's probably the reason we don't see buzzards at a road kill like we used to.

As to fire ants, I greet them with mixed emotions. I know that it hurts to get stung. I will accept the fact that baby calves and fawns have been blinded and even killed by them, but on the other hand look what they have done for us. Can you remember the last time you had to dig a seed tick out of one of your kids or doctored a chigger bit? The fire ant is responsible for this. I'll take a fire ant sting or two in lieu of getting eaten by ticks and chiggers. The Lord works in wondrous ways.

The fire ant has been blamed for the demise of the bob white quail in East Texas. I am sure they didn't help any, but they are not to blame. The reason is loss of habitat. There is nothing here for them to eat. Very few thing can live off of pine trees and coastal Bermuda grass. Example, the King Ranch in South Texas had one of the greatest population of bob white quail in the country and lots of fire ants. Please don't get the impression that I welcome fire ants, but I will still take them over seed ticks and chiggers. If they could talk I bet the dogs, cats, cattle, and other wildlife would agree.

The squirrels are another creature that has come to town, and I mean a bunch of them. I can look out my window any morning and see more squirrels in fifteen minutes than I could see in a whole season when I was a kid. As I have mentioned before people used to eat them. Old squirrels in dumplings, young squirrels fried.

I remember a squirrel hunting experience I had when I first got in the army in WWII. I was first stationed in Camp Bowie in Brownwood, Texas. The camp was located close to Pecan Bayou which had lots of squirrels up and down it. There was a boy in my outfit whose parents lived on the Bayou, and Dutch took me home with him one weekend.

That afternoon his Mother told us to go down on the Bayou and kill a mess of squirrels for supper. He took a 22 rifle from the rack and handed me one. I thought to myself even Annie Oakely couldn't hit a running fox squirrel with a rifle, but I didn't say anything. He told me to take the first shot.

I blasted away at the first one hitting it behind the front legs. When Dutch picked it up he threw it away telling me it was not only an old squirrel, but it wasn't shot in the head. He said his mama would have a fit if we brought in anything except young squirrels shot in the head. We carried home a big mess of young fox squirrels all shot in the head.

His mother fried the young squirrel in butter served with cream gravy and hot biscuits. It was the best meal that I had eaten in a long time. I know having eaten Army cooking for a year had something to do with it, and after more than sixty three years, I still rate it one of the best meals that I ever had.

Snakes and Other Varmints

When I was a kid growing up in East Texas snakes were a part of our every day life. They were around the house in the form of chicken snakes and copperheads with and occasional coach whip sighted. Chicken snakes mainly around the hen house trying to get eggs and baby chicks.

A trip to the woods would encounter spead'en adders (puff adders), bull snakes, coral snakes, many coach whips, water snakes, and the dangerous cotton mouth moccasin. Some of folks said that a coach whip could form a loop and roll along fast enough to catch a running boy. Of course nobody really believed this but it made a good story.

I have always had a thing about snakes and used to catch them and bring them home. I got broken of this habit at an early age when I proudly brought home what I thought was a large chicken snake that was coiled around my arm and found out it was a copperhead.

I went a great number of years that I didn't see many snakes, especially in town or dead along the road like we used to. When we moved to our house more than thirty years ago the houses on each side of us were vacant and none had been built behind us. We used to see quail possums, coons, rabbits fox, and lots of rats, but no snakes. I have seen three this year.

I have never been afraid of snakes like some people, consequently I have been the unofficial snake disposal man in my circle of friends. This had been brought about by absentee husbands or husbands standing helpless on a chair waiting for help.

A few years ago I made two trips out to a friend's house to get rid of chicken snakes that were eating their little love birds which they kept in an atrium attached to the house. Then, out to my son's house where the snakes were eating up our pigeons. Got rid of several out there.

One night a back door neighbor called to say one had crawled in her door. Of course her husband was out of town. I doubt he would have been of much help if he had been there. We found it under a couch. As I was in the process of getting rid of it she stood poised with a hoe ready to chop it up. I told her that it would mess up the carpet and she retorted "To heck with the carpet." That one was a copperhead.

A similar thing happened at the Methodist Church where the ladies were preparing food in the kitchen. A chicken snake crawled up on the patio near the door. I didn't have to remove this one because one of the little ladies beat it to death with a broom handle, before I could do anything. Then there was the hilariously funny episode that happened to a close friend, whose name I won't mention. He has a mounted bass over the door to his office. A little bird hatched a brood of chicks in the mouth of the fish. A chicken snake raided the nest and then took up residence in a straw hat hanging by the door. The friend came in, and put the hat on his head, snake and all. Understand it made a terrible mess of his office.

Got another call from the wife at the same place saying she had a snake in her kitchen. I raced out as fast as I could and was glad to see her out in the yard. I was afraid the way she talked that it was trying to eat her. Finally found the little ten inch creature and got rid of it.

One more trip to the ranch to get rid of one that had gotten into the quail pen and swallowed five eggs.

I have mentioned having seen only a few snakes in my years in this house. A few weeks ago during the cool, cloudy weather I stepped out of my shop and there was a copperhead crawling by. Before I could react it turned around and crawled through a hole in the wall back into my shop. We haven't met since.

Then another recent call from my neighbors that a snake was crawling up their wall. It was a chicken snake that was trying to reach a bird nest in a hanging basket. Took care of that.

I have been talking about chicken snakes. I think their official name is rat snakes. They will always be chicken snakes to me. They do some good by catching rats but they also do some harm by raiding bird and squirrel nest. I remember one time out at the Boy's and Girl's club we were sitting under a tree and heard a loud thump and saw a snake on the ground wrapped around a baby squirrel. About this time the snake turned loose and the squirrel raced back up the tree.

One of my most memorable snake episode included my youngest son who was deathly afraid of snakes. We traveled a lot and he would mow the grass for me. Back then I was trying to grow blueberries in wooden barrels.

I was having trouble with birds and I put a rubber snake in one of the bushes and failed to tell him about it. When I got home the rubber snake and the blueberry bush were beaten to a pulp with an ax handle almost ruined in the process.

Most people are afraid of snakes and wish there were none around. It could be much worse. Since they have no legs they move slowly and are easy to avoid. Just think if the snake had not talked Eve into eating the apple, they would now have legs and no telling what we would be up against.

Buying a New Car

So you have convinced yourself, along with some 16 million people nation wide, that you need a new car. The reasons are many. Although your car is in reasonably good shape it probably could use a set of tires, a battery, and a tune up. Since it requires cash to get this done and you don't have the money, that is one excuse for getting a new one. Then there are the many discounts and cash back plans available. But perhaps the biggest selling point is the "forever payment plan," where by if you don't live long enough your grandchildren can pay it off.

If you have done your shopping you have by now realized that there is not much difference in the make of cars in the same price range or finance terms offered. So your next choice is whether to buy out of town or from a local dealer. Today you have three local dealers to choose from. How about ten to choose from? That's how many we had in Crockett right after WWII.

For a Ford car or a pickup you would go to Sullivan Motor Company owned by Buck Sullivan. It was located on Houston Ave. where Barkley Mortuary is now. Although they didn't keep them in stock you could order an Edsel. Wade Sullivan says he doesn't remember them ever selling one.

Chevrolet cars and trucks could be had through the King Motor Company owned by the Robert King family. It was located where the Lucas Roofing Company is now. You could also buy a Cadillac from them.

Chryslers were available at Knox Motor Co. It was owned by Leo Knox and Later by W. H. Knox. It was originally located in a building behind the First National Bank. Later on it took on Plymouths and International pickups and moved to South Fourth, St. where Wayne Williams Motor Co. is now located.

What about a new DeSota, Plymouth, Willis Jeep, GMC pickup, Studebaker car, or an Oliver Tractor? George Childs was the man to see. His dealership was located on South Fourth, St. where the Ronald Hill garage is located.

A Pontiac with an Indian Chief on the radiator cap could be had from Jack Barbee Motor Co. According to Jack Neal Barbee its original location was close to where the Dollar Store is now and later in the building vacated by Knox Motor Co.

Bob Wray Motor Co. was the Buick Agency. It was located in the building formerly occupied by Knox Motor Co. and Barbee Motors. It was later acquired by Louie Piazza.

Denny Collins had the Lincoln-Mercury and Ford Tractor dealership and it was located on West Goliad where the new bed and breakfast and restaurant is set to open soon.

If you wanted to take Lucille for a ride in a Merry Oldsmobile you would visit the Benny Ellis Motor Co.

located across from the First Methodist Church on Goliad. Benny stayed pretty busy selling cars, insurance, and raising four pretty daughters.

The Jim Ulrich dealership building was built by Dub Issac that sold GMC trucks and later Pontiac, Oldsmoblile, and Buick. It was later acquired by Jeff Sewell and then by Vernon Wilson, and Jim Ulrich.

Perhaps a Nash Rambler fitted your budget. If so the O.B. Rhone Motor Co. was the place to go. It was located where the Hadid Grocery building is on South Fourth, St. He also sold Avery tractors.

Although you had many dealers to choose from back then you didn't have the incentives that are offered today. You either paid cash or arranged your own financing though a national lending agency or from a local bank. Back then our two local banks weren't looking for car loans. These two banks had survived the Great Depression by being ultra conservative and only loaning to people who could prove that they didn't need the money.

It's a different ball game today. Every lending agency is offering every incentive to finance a car for you. The one thing that hasn't changed is that you still have to make the payments.

Okay you have by now thought this out and have your Credit Card debt in hand, have Health Insurance, have money for your children's education put aside, and a few months salary saved in case you lose your job, so you are ready to take the big step. Where to buy? Good judgment would cause you to pick someone close by for your warranty service, someone who pays City, County, and School taxes, someone who supports every worth while project in the Community, including the Boy's and Girl's Club, our Scout program, the Civic Center, the Little League program, our Chamber of Commerce, the Library and the many other worth while projects that come along. That someone is your local car dealer.

Probably by now you have learned more about buying a new car than you wanted to, so with that, we hope you make a good deal and drive it safely.

Staying in the Hospital

Each time that I pass our beautiful modern hospital I feel a sense of pride. Pride because we worked so hard to get the first one here. We didn't even have the land and no money when it first began but with a sense of Community pride, and everyone working together it was accomplished.

We were more fortunate than some towns our size because we had two clinics owned and operated by dedicated doctors. What they lacked in modern equipment they more than made up for, with knowledge and common sense acquired by years of experience.

Back then Lufkin, Nacogdoches, and even Tyler didn't have the modern hospitals that they have today. That left Houston or Dallas for us to turn to. Since Houston was nearer and in our trade territory that's where most of our doctors sent us.

I had occasion lately to spend a few days in our hospital with an infected leg wound. From the moment I checked in I was impressed with the efficiency and courtesy of the admitting personnel. I was given a wheel chair ride down to room 127, where thank God, I was allowed to get into my own pajamas instead of one those gowns that open down the back and bares everything but your soul to everyone who comes in.

I was put in a bed that had every gadget on it that you could imagine. You could push a button and adjust your bed to any position that you wanted. Buttons that worked the light, a button to summons a nurse, and a handy telephone attached to the bed within easy reach that didn't fall on the floor when you reached for it. And of course television controls handy.

I noticed when I entered the room that it was cold enough in there to kill a hog. I mentioned to the little orderly that wheeled me down to the room to adjust the controls, that the unit was blowing cold air on me. She said that there were only four adjustments on the unit and that was off, on, hot, or cold.

I thought well she just doesn't know how to adjust the thing so I mentioned this to the nice nurse that came in and she verified this. I asked her if I could change rooms and she assured me that all the rooms were the same. I asked her if this had been reported and she said many times. It didn't take a rocket scientist to see what the problem was. Number one, the heating and cooling unit was placed in the wrong place, which was right even and the same height as the patient's bed. The second mistake was putting fixed louvers on the units that directs the air right on the patient.

Later on, my mind was diverted from freezing when a nice young, I guess nurse, came in to ask me some questions. I was asked questions about my personal life that went back to the beginning. Questions that my Mother never asked me. Since Peggy was sitting there I didn't really lie, but I told the truth five or six different ways to some of the questions.

I got to know some of the nurses quite well especially the ones who came in every few hours to take my temperature, and blood pressure, I enjoyed the visit every morning at four a.m., with the people who spoke very little English, who drew blood from me. It helped while the time away at night to listen to the conversations of the night shift nurses, recounting their experiences of the day.

Back to the cold room, I finally told the nurses that something had to be done. They said that they knew exactly what to do, that they had to do it for almost every patient. They proceeded to tape a pillowslip across the louvers to divert the cold air. Now can you imagine this? A multi-million dollar hospital equipped with the latest computer technology, staffed with well trained personnel, with the latest of everything, with a pillow slip taped over the air conditioner to keep a patient from freezing. As I lay there, I realized that I had the same problem when I was a patient many years ago.

I also thought how simple it would be to correct this problem. A three or four foot piece of Plexiglas or even plywood, with two vertical slots, fastened to the unit with two set screws would allow the air to be diverted toward the ceiling instead of the patient.

One must assume that for a condition like this to exist all these years that none of the administrative personnel, or any of the directors have ever spent a night freezing their tail off in one of the rooms. When that happens you can bet that something will be done especially if they stay in room 217.

This Too Shall Pass

I believe in this old Biblical Passage, especially as it pertains to Presidential Elections, I should be accustomed to them because I have lived under sixteen Presidents. Certainly I don't remember all of them but I can recall fourteen of them.

I was born during Woodrow Wilson's term. The man who devoted his life to forming "The League Of Nations." The purpose was to end all wars. Congress rejected it.

I don't remember anything about Warren Harding's term. I guess I was being weaned during that time.

I remember some events during Calvin Coolidge's term. My father worked on a road construction crew that built the road between Palestine and Frankston. We lived in a tent city that moved with the work. He drove a four-mule team that pulled a grader with mules as big as elephants. My Mother says I picked up profanity at an early age. I vividly remember having my mouth washed out with soap.

We moved once during Herbert Hoover's tenure where I entered first grade twice. I guess everyone of my age can remember the Stock Market Crash of 1929 when millions of people lost their jobs and the savings of a life time. When some committed suicide rather than face the consequences. It is burned in my memory, because my Father lost his job.

Then came the Messiah, Franklin D. Roosevelt, who uttered the most reassuring words since "Give me liberty or give me death," when he said, "The only thing we have to fear is fear itself." Those words, the jaunty tilt of his cigarette holder, and his theme song of "Happy Day's are here again," was just the tonic a beaten people needed. He started many innovative projects, among the most successful being the Civilian Conservation Corps, called the C.C.C. program whereby able bodied young men, many from farms, were brought into semi military environment and put to work doing worth while projects. They were paid thirty dollars a month with twenty-five of this sent home to their parents. My father got a job with them.

Then we had eight years of Dwight Eisenhower who was a brilliant military commander and was just the man during a period of calm when we didn't expect our President to do much.

Then the days of Camelot with John Kennedy and Jackie, the beautiful people. Days filled with hope that we could live in a different world that was cut short by a psycho's bullet.

Along came Lyndon Johnson, the crude, over bearing one who's idea of grandeur and a place in posterity and who was the author of the "Great Society" program that got carried away with its self and did more harm than good. That too has not passed.

The paranoid one, Richard Nixon, came and went and left us a different people, not the good either.

Gerald Ford was thrust into office, where to his credit he did no harm. Not much good either as far as that goes.

Jimmy Carter, a good man, of course being a good man is better than being a bad man, but the world is full of good men who can't get the job done. Twenty percent inflation is a legacy hard to live down.

Ronald Reagan, "Bed Time For Bonzo," the great communicator, who brought a sense of decency to the office, who took credit for bringing down the Berlin Wall, but who should go down in history as the President who defied the Air Traffic Controllers and fired them for going on strike. That sent a lasting message to the Labor Unions that has helped us to this day.

George Herbert Walker Bush, a man who had the courage and skill to free Kuwait and who really should have had a second term where he could have done this Country lots of good.

William J. Clinton, a man who brought a truck load of low morals from Arkansas and installed them in the White House. We are lucky that he didn't have a son to pass the legacy on to but unlucky that he has an ambitious wife that we have to contend with.

That brings us down to Dubya. You may not agree with what he wants, but he seems to know what he wants. That's more than a lot of people know. Like Roosevelt after the Crash of '29, he gave us confidence after 911. Of course there are something's that I don't agree with him on, but one thing we do agree on is his opposition to Homosexual (some call them Gay) marriages.

With that I will close, before I get sick to my stomach. I have lived too long.

DON'T BLAME THE SYSTEM

School days, school days, dear old Golden Rule days, reading and writing, and rithmetic taught to the tune of a hickory stick, you were my queen in calico, I was your bashful barefoot beau, and you wrote on my slate, "I love you Joe," when we were a couple of kids.

A wave of nostalgia sweeps over me when I recite these lines. Although by the time I came along the slate had been replaced by a lined writing tablet and the hickory stick replaced by a wooden paddle. I can still relate to those days of innocence.

The student body made up of kids from and ethnic neighborhood. No school buses, no cafeteria, no vending machines, and the few cars on the grounds belonged to the teachers.

Assembly every morning, with prayer, the Pledge of Allegiance, and most remembered the songs we sang. After more than eighty years I can still remember most of them. We don't sing enough now days, we let someone else do it for us. There should be more singing in our homes, our schools, and certainly more in our Church services.

What a change in my life time. The writing tablet replaced by a computer, the wooden paddle replaced by a book on Child psychology, which some think contributes to the loss of discipline today, and with the student body composed of children from every ethnic background.

Our forefathers who wrote our Constitution, in a noble gesture, stated that all men are created equal. However noble the gesture we know now that this is not true. We are created with certain genes that are passed on to our offspring's.

Some are born short, some tall, some strong, some weak, some fast, some slow, some white, some black, some yellow, and so forth. It is evident that some are born with a greater ability to learn than others. We realize that this ability to learn is a gift that every parent should utilize in order to prepare the child for the years ahead.

Sadly, today, this is not the case. Children are being sent to our schools born out of wedlock as advertised by their parents, saddled with unpronounceable names, derived from no known language, and with absolutely no parental training at home. All with the expectation that the school system can make up for what they missed at home.

There is enough blame to go around. When the spoiled brats of the so called, affluent, segment of our society are added to the mix it creates almost a hopeless situation that is causing many of our qualified teachers to quit the profession.

What have we let happen to us? Some want to blame integration. That happened more than two generations ago and the chaos and disruption that it caused should have abated some by now. Immigrants? Certainly not being able to speak English is a handicap. Lack of money?

We have always had that problem. Teachers? The majority of our teachers are well qualified and dedicated to their job.

In talking to teachers, administrators, and even students, from both public and private schools, the main problem is defined as lack of early discipline in the home. Discipline is defined as, "Instruction and exercise designed to train to proper conduct or action." A board or paddle is not mentioned.

A solution to the problem will not come easily. All the promises out of Washington of Vouchers, or the "No child left behind program," and other schemes will not get the job done.

There must be a practical solution found. It must be, our future depends on it. My generation cannot be depended on to solve it. We are too embedded with the twin evils of hypocrisy and apathy to get the job done. It's up to another generation to find a solution.

If we could recall the discipline of our childhood and put it into practice today, that would be good, but if bringing it back also brought back milking cows, drawing water, and toting wood, that would be bad. The twin evils rear their heads again.

There's a County and Western song that is topping the charts today, it is sung by an old boy who has long hair, and needs a shave, but it conveys a message when he sings, "What say you? What say you?" Good question. What do you say?

On Being Sick

Right around Xmas I began to have a shortness of breath and a tightening sensation in by chest. I diagnosed it as a chest cold. With these symptoms came a dry hacking cough. I didn't think much about it because we have all had these aliments in our past, and could always shake it off in a few days. My friends offered some home remedies, such as a daily vitamin tablet, zinc tablet, calcium tablet, pineapple juice, orange juice, an onion a day, plus many more of these home remedies were offered.

The Hispanic lady who helps Peggy had a whole handful of solutions, delivered in her native tongue which neither of us understands. One word that I did catch was the word "Tequila." That reminded me of an experience that we had many years ago.

Back in our naïve days we thought we ought to take the "Copper Canyon Tour" which requires us to drive to Presidio, Texas and to Chihuahua, Mexico, where we embarked on a primitive train from Chihuahua to Los Mochas on the West coast of Mexico.

About halfway to Los Mochas, on top of the Sierra Madre mountains there is a halfway stop with primitive cabins, a restaurant, with a generator system for electricity. After dinner we were sitting around outside our cabins when Peggy developed one of her famous sore throat and flu symptoms. We were discussing what we could do when a nice looking young Spaniard sitting near us approached us and said he had overheard the conversation and that he was a Doctor and could give her a shot of penicillin. When she told him that she was very allergic to penicillin he said the next best thing was tequila. He told me to give her a double shot of tequila every two hours, chased with lemon, during the night.

I did this and since I didn't want to catch what she had I took a couple of shots myself, just to be sure. The next morning she woke as fit as a fiddle, while I woke up with a hang over that would make history. However I must admit that I have tried the tequila remedy this go round with few results with the exception of the hangover that seems to go with the treatment.

As a last resort I went to my doctor, who after x-rays, blood work, and breathing test, decided I had chest congestion caused by fluid on my lungs. I thought then that he would prescribe a mustard plaster on my chest, inhale heated Vick Salve, breathe some hot sulfur fumes and maybe prescribe other remedies that used to work.

I was sent home with Albuterol inhalation aerosol to be used four times a day, potassium cloride, one each day, and a little pill of Furosemide, which is a diuretic. Now diuretic translated into East Texas language means "don't get far from a restroom." Still suspect heart congestion.

Back to the Doctor. Came home with sulfamethoxazole/tmp tablets, two a day. A new inhalant called Advair, twice a day. Continue the little dynamite pill and stay close to a restroom or a cow shed or a secluded spot some where. Heart congestion still suspected.

To another Doctor, whose conclusion was a bad cold with flu symptoms. After more x-rays, blood work, and EKG, there was then some doubt about congestive heart problems. Results sent to heart specialist who concurs with the diagnoses. However he ordered an Echo Cardiogram to be done the next week.

In the meantime the chest cold has broken with great discharges of fluid from the lungs and nasal passages, just as it has always done. I am doing better every day. May be I will reach a normal state of health if there is such a thing anymore.

There is one redeeming factor in this whole episode. I lost about ten pounds. Whether it was from the medicine or the exercise of running to the restroom, whatever, it is gone. I would like to keep it off, but not if I have to go through with this mess again.

The next time I catch one of these things I know what I will do. I will use the mustard plaster, Vick salve, bananas, Zinc tablets, calcium tablets, sulfur, onion and the tequila treatment and save a bunch of time and money.

On second thought I will probably go back and see a doctor.

Social Security Or
Insecurity?

Just about everything you read and hear lately is about Social Security. Whether it is going broke and when that might be. Some, including the President, believe it should be fixed. Some believe that it should be left alone, while some don't know, and many don't care.

Millions don't have a dog in the fight, so to speak, this includes members of my generation who are rounding third and heading home and who have been assured that any change will not affect us. Most of my generation have been in the program from the beginning I got my card in June of 1937. Early on common sense dictated that Social Security benefits alone would not be enough to provide for our retirement so many of us saved and invested for the future.

Then you have the members of congress who piously lament the plight of the poor retiree when they are set for life with their full salary and health benefits that continue after they retire. Add to the mix the federal employees, most who have fed from the public trough down through the years and who have an excellent retirement program. With the addition of State, municipal, school, retired military, plus others with business retirement programs, you further add to those who don't have a dog in the fight.

I saw an article that suggested Congress put everyone in the same boat by cashing out their and the federal employees retirement funds and putting that money into the social security pot and then let them try to get by on Social Security benefits alone.

The President's solution is to have some of each workers contribution invested in the stock market. Of course one big problem is where will the big hunk of money come from to get it started. Another problem, and one that concerns many of us, is who will handle this money? The President believes that the average American is capable of handling his own investments.

Does the President include the average American family who owes more than $9,000. in credit card debt, with many just making the minimum payment and paying up to 20% interest on the balance or, on our so called bright college kids who have four or more credit cards, and who spend an average of $4,368.00 per year, with delinquent credit card balance of $2,226.00 and paying up to 27% interest on the unpaid balance?

Or the gullible ones who fall for the Debt Consolidation pitch and just get deeper in debt. Should we consider the ones who use the Payday Lenders and pay interest rates that reach 780%? Is there any help for those who borrow on their homes to satisfy their spending habits? Should we ignore the Growing number of people who dodge their debts by taking personal bankruptcy?

Getting down to the State level. Could we remotely trust the more than half of our Texas citizens who average spending over $44.00 per month on the lottery with the poorer less educated bearing the biggest burden? Broken down into race shows whites spending $30.76 per month, Hispanic $64.83, and blacks $89.00 or over $1,000.00 per year.

Can those people be helped? Is there anyway that you could get over to them what compound interest is. That this $1,000.00 per year, invested wisely would grow to over $1,00,000.00 in thirty years?

To further belabor the point about the dog in the fight you must include the millions who are wards of the government, with food stamps, housing, and free medical care. They know that regardless of what happens to social security that their situation will not change now or ever.

So that leaves us wondering who is for this change. There is no question that savings invested in the market will out perform the return on Social Security, and that younger people will come out much better under this program. If a sensible way can be found to make this change then the young wage earners should get behind it.

You can't blame all the ills of this country on the people. Some blame must be shared by the ones who promote the mentality of spend now and pay later, and don't worry about tomorrow.

The credit card companies like the tobacco industry know that if you hook them young enough you have them for life. That's why they are introducing a Kitty Card. What next? A prenatal card?

I received a platinum card in the mail the other day which promised me the moon. I thought wow how it shined and how impressive it would look being swiped through a card machine.

When I read the fine print about what it would cost me, my old blue Visa card looked pretty good and the old axiom of "If it ain't broke, don't fix it" came back to me and I threw the pretty card in the trash.

Bar-B-Que Then & Now

The word bar-b-que is about the most misused work in our language today. Its original definition is found in The American College Dictionary as being "large or political gathering, usually in the open air, where animals are roasted whole."

There are many versions of how it got started. One version has it that one of our cave man ancestors threw an animal on the fire to burn the hair off and left it too long and discovered bar-b-que. There are still some primitive tribes who practice this.

Old Arthur had a secret way to make the toughest meat tenderand retain the flavor. He would put the meat on the pit for awhile, then steam it in its own juices, then back on the pit. His simple sauce was red pepper, chili powder, and vinegar.

I have eaten good bar-b-que at many of the places mentioned in Texas Highways, and Texas Monthly among being, Joe Allen's in Abilene, Pereini's in Buffalo Gap, Kruze's Market in Lockhart, Cooper's in Llano and in Mason including our good bar-b-que places here in Crockett.

Of all the places I have eaten, I believe year in and year out the best brisket I have ever eaten is served by Louie Muellers in Taylor, Texas. We started eating there fifty years ago when we first started deer hunting in the Hill Country.

Louie got started in a tin building, with only screens for windows, and a dirt floor covered with saw dust. There was a pit and a counter. Your meat was weighed and placed on butcher paper. A loaf of bread, a pile of unpeeled onions, and a jar of pickles completed the menu choice.

You sat at a bench type table with army surplus knives chained to the table and the sauce, which they called gravy, was a bottle of vinegar and red pepper. Years later they moved across the street to a larger building.

Like Arthur Hatch, they had a procedure to tenderize the brisket. I got acquainted with the old man who cooked the meat and he told me how they did it. They started about three in the morning with eight to ten pound briskets, rolled in rock salt and course ground pepper. The meat was cooked over coals, (no smoking fire) until about eight the next morning, then wrapped in unwaxed butcher paper, put back on the pit and allowed to slow cook until lunch time. Each order was weighed and served on butcher paper. Their sauce was vinegar, red pepper, and chili powder. You never saw any tomatoes or tomato sauce used on meat around any of those places.

There are many self proclaimed bar-b-que experts today, in every kind of get up, cooking on everything from wash tubs to elaborate bar-b-que contraptions, using every kind of wood, with various kinds of meat, with exotic sauce recipes, all to create a dish that can't hold a candle to that chicken cooked on the open pit long, long ago.

Trinity River Authority – Fifty Years of Service

A long time dream of Dallas and Fort Worth leaders was navigation of the Trinity River. A long time nightmare of the railroads was that this would come about which would reduce their freight rates.

This dream had long been promoted by the Trinity River Improvement Association. Among its boosters was an odd character calling himself Commodore Hatfield who used to make the trip by barge from Liberty to Dallas always stopping at the lock and dam.

In the past, barge traffic could reach Dallas and Fort Worth but not on a reliable basis. In fact, Darsey's store in Grapeland used to receive goods shipped by barge which was unloaded at Alabama Crossing.

To ever make even shallow barge traffic on the river possible, a series of Lock and Dams had to be built. One of the first started but never finished was the one near Midway.

Peggy's, maternal Grandfather, Uncle Ed Arnold, remembered when it was constructed and told me about it. A railroad spur was built from Crockett to haul the materials. One time a train with a load of dynamite tried to run through a forest fire and the dynamite exploded.

Oddly, the partial construction of the Lock and Dam virtually stopped all traffic because it blocked the up river passage except during flood stage. It also blocked the fish from going up river during low water.

To get anything done, an Authority had to be created by the Texas Legislature. It was imperative that the bill should be introduced by the Senator who represented the Counties in the basin.

This Senator was reluctant to sponsor the bill because she was beholden to the railroads. I got my first look at raw politics when I went along with a group of powerful men that met with her when she was told, in no uncertain manner, that if she didn't sponsor the bill they would beat her in the next election.

She sponsored the bill and the Legislature created the Authority. The legislation provided no funds, nor taxing authority. The Trinity Improvement Association provided the start up money.

The Master Plan called for the creation of a barge Canal from Anahuac to the East side of Fort Worth. A series of large lakes would reduce some of the canal work on the river. The bond election held for this purpose was defeated in 1973

If it had passed we would have seen a vast industrial complex created along the river, creating jobs, and furnishing much needed tax money for our county.

The central irony of TRA's history is that although it was not successful in creating navigation on the river it had evolved into one of the largest providers of wholesale water and waste water related services in the southwest and has done so without the benefit of a tax base or appropriations from the state or federal government. With the result that today, it has over a billion dollars in assets.

The board consists of twenty four directors appointed for six year terms by the governor. It is very efficient with an excellent staff and five standing committees each headed by a director.

Each item of business is thoroughly researched by the staff, endorsed by a committee, and submitted to each director prior to a board meeting. The board meetings are all business with an agenda with as many as fifty items covered in two hours or less.

Houston County has had only five directors in fifty years. Quite unusual to say the least. First was Sam Arledge, then Alvis Story, myself, Jake Caprielian, and the present director Ed Hargett.

Attending those very efficient board meetings for eighteen years has made me reluctant to attend some of local meetings that have no planned agenda, no orderly course of action, and which allows attendees to ramble on and on and in many cases, completely off the subject.

Now I have no objection to rambling when telling a long winded tale, or when trying to explain something to Peggy, but not at a meeting.

Time to Live-Time to Die

In doing some of my articles in the past I have tried to inject a sense of humor in them. However, I can find no humor to inject in this article concerning the drama being played out down Florida.

It's a sad case involving a young woman's right to live or die. A decision that should be made by the ones closest to her. Instead it has turned into a circus by the media, and others who have no business interfering in this matter.

We have long known that there are more clowns in Washington than in a circus. Some of the clowns in congress recently proved that you can put on a show even without makeup. These shameless people played out an act of showmanship, when they made a special trip back to Washington, from one of their many long holidays, and passed a bill that plainly interfered with the rights of those involved in this case. And to further demonstrate what a politician will stoop to, our President interrupted an outing at the ranch to make a quick overnight trip to Washington on his "flying hotel" at a cost of thousand of dollars, to sign the bill in the middle of the night. Talk about grandstanding!

I admit I have been critical of both parties in this sad case. I can't side with the husband because he could have removed himself from the case long ago by divorcing her. Nobody would have blamed him. But apparently he has waited it out in the hopes of getting some money when she dies. Also by having two children with another woman doesn't gain him any points.

As to the parents, they have been completely unreasonable about the whole thing. I cannot understand how any parent could let a daughter suffer this long with no hope of recovery. I wouldn't treat an animal like that.

I have a habit of expressing myself, sometimes very forcibly. I have, had some tell me that if you have never been in a situation like this you don't know what you would do. Oh, but I have.

Our first child was born a "Blue Baby" and couldn't walk at twenty months of age. A Houston doctor told us that there was no hope that he would make it. To take him home and have another child. We were crushed by the news as we returned to his little brother at home.

A second doctor, fresh out of Medical School, thought he could be helped by an operation. When we handed a frightened young boy to a nurse at the door of the operating room we were told that he would either come out of the operating room able to lead a normal life or he wouldn't come out at all. That's just the way we wanted it. There was no discussion about bringing him home to die a slow death. We faced it again, thought not as seriously, when he was thirteen and they went back into his heart to further enable him to live a normal life.

The Lord wasn't quite through with us, and our youngest son suffered a massive stroke that left him brain dead. The finest doctors available said that he would never recover and would be on life support until he died.

His wife and daughters made the decision, which we whole heartily agreed with, to withdraw his life support system. Sure it was tough to tell him goodbye, but this was the only sensible choice.

Yes friends it was tough. I just hope someone loves me enough to do the same for me when my time comes. You could ask nothing better than to have your loved ones all say goodbye to you.

Stand on Whiskey

I see that the recent Local Option Election held in Latexo failed to pass by a small margin. This kind of election creates a lot of mixed emotions in the people involved.

On the positive side it would have created a great deal of revenue for the City, schools, and the County. In the thoughts of some people it would have been seen as approving the consumption of alcohol. It was almost a no win situation.

I have been associated with alcohol one way or another all my life. I have been told that my grandfather used it, my father used and abused it all his life, and I have used it off and on all my life, sometimes in moderation, and sometime not.

My first taste of it was in my teens when we lived in a country town with no movies or any other form of recreation, with preachers from both churches preaching "hell fire and damnation" for anyone who used it. We would buy so called "boot legged whiskey" from the makers served up in fruit jars. During WWII, we country boys were introduced to mixed drinks, served not only in bars, but in the homes we were invited into.

After the War most of us who used it got married, had children, and we cut down on our use of it. Not so much for moral reasons, but because we could not afford to buy it. Getting it involved a trip to Trinity County. I don't know how much the effect on us would have been if we could have bought it locally.

Crockett has had one local option election , since I have been here. It raised a great hue and cry, mainly in our Churches, about the evils of alcohol. Much of this opposition was fueled by the Trinity County liquor industry which poured more than $100,000.00 into the effort to defeat this proposal. Much of this money went into some local Church coffers and perhaps into some local pockets.

As I grow older I find myself using alcohol more and more on a regular basis partly because I can afford to buy it and because my doctors who use it themselves say it is good for me. At any rate that's my excuse.

I guess the best stand on whiskey was given in a speech by an old East Texas lawyer who was running for the Texas Legislature who was asked by a reporter how he stood on whiskey? His reply, "If when you say whiskey you mean the devil's brew, the poison scourge, the bloody monster that defiles innocence, dethrones reason, creates misery and despair, yes, literally takes the bread out of the mouth of babies, if you mean that vile drink that topples the Christian man and woman from the pinnacles of gracious righteous living into the bottomless pit of shame and despair, helplessness and hopelessness, then I am against it.

But if, when you say whiskey, you mean that oil of conversation, you mean that philosophic drink which is consumed when good fellows get together, which puts a song in their hearts, laughter on their lips, and a smile of contentment in their eyes, if you mean Christmas cheer, if you mean that stimulating drink which puts the spring in an old mans step on a frosty morning, if you mean that drink which permits a man to magnify his joys and happiness and to forget, if only for a moment, life's tragedies and sorrows, if you mean that drink which pours into our Treasury untold millions with which to provide tender care for the crippled children, our aged and infirm, and to build schools, hospitals, and roads...then I am for it."

My feelings on this subject are just about those of an old boy who desperately needed a job during the depression and applied for a job teaching science at a country school.

One of the board members in an attempt to impress the other members asked the boy if he believed in Devine Creation or Evolution. The boy replied, "I can teach it either way."

Yesterday and Possum Hunting

I saw a TV program the other night about a boy and his dad possum hunting. A wave of nostalgia swept over me and it took be back to my yearling days as a boy in a Northeast Texas town where I spent some of the better days of my young life.

Days when you kicked off you shoes in the spring frolicking like a young colt not having to put them on again until frost. Summer days spent in the fields and woods wearing nothing but a pair of overalls, eating wild plums, blackberries, watermelons, and plenty of peas, cornbread , and sweet milk for dinner and supper.

The fall days brought on shoes and a shirt under the overalls. A different menu of musky dimes, chinquapins, black haws, hickory nuts, bull nettle kernels, and small sweet potatoes left in the field, and by all means persimmons. Nothing better than a ripe persimmon that frost had sweetened. Nothing worst than a green one. After you had eaten one you cracked the seeds to see if you got a knife, fork or spoon. You older people know what I am talking about, I don't have enough space to explain it to you younger ones. The ripe persimmons brought out the possums that loved them more than we did. This brings us to the point of this story.

We used to catch possums and sell them. Now many of you young people probably believe that possums are born dead by the side of the road. But people back then knew better and believed that a possum surrounded by sweet potatoes slowly baked in a wood stove oven was about the best food on earth.

The daddy of one of our gang had a possum dog. I don't mean a cur dog cross that would chase a possum, but a treeing Walker Hound that could cold trail a possum up a tree with a voice that could be heard for miles on a still frosty night. When he treed in a small tree one of us would climb up and shake him out for the dog to catch. If the tree was too tall we could usually knock him out with one of our, for want of a better word, rock shooters. The possums were put in a cage and fattened on sweet potatoes and sold.

Our world was shattered when the dog was sold. That left us no alternative but to find them in their dens. We knew every hollow in the woods and we would visit them. If the scrapped off hairs were pointed inward the possum was home. To make sure a sharpened stick was jammed in the holler if he was there he would make a noise. The next move was to smoke him out with a fire of damp leaves. If this failed to get him he had to be twisted out. This called for a long stick with a sharpened ford on the end. The trick was to jam the stick in his hide and twist until it took hold and pull him out. It worked sometime. Some one asked if it was painful and it really wasn't unless the stick broke and you jabbed yourself in the stomach.

One Saturday morning two of us needed twenty cents to go to the picture show that afternoon. Since we pretty near knew where a possum would likely be, we took off for the woods. Sure enough he was home. We had to twist him out. In doing so we took off a big patch of hair on one side. We went ahead and skinned him out and took him to the produce house and got our twenty cents. Now the hides were sold with the hair side in and the produce man didn't notice the missing hair. Later he did and that ended our possum hide business.

I got a job delivering papers and soon after we made another of our frequent moves, following the job, to a small town that offered almost nothing for a growing boy. With that move I left my joyous boyhood behind, never to be regained, and moved into manhood too early. Nothing left of those days but precious memories.

In the Army

You're in the army now,
You're not behind the plough,
You'll never get rich,
A digging a ditch,
You're in the army now.

Back in 1940 when I decided to join the Army I wasn't digging ditches, but it was just as bad. I had a menial job with no future. I thought anything was better than that, plus the fact that I would have been drafted, when I reach twenty-one. So I joined up. A WWII recruiting slogan claimed, "That every day in the army was like Sunday on the farm." Now it wasn't quite like that, but it still beat what I had been doing.

I joined a National Guard Unit in Winnsboro, Texas where I had relatives. The uniforms and weapons were WWI vintage as were the officers, and the training methods. That changed in November when the National Guard was federalized and we were all in the regular army. In November 1940, we were shipped to Camp Bowie in Brownwood, Texas where we became part of the old 36th division.

Now the Defense Department had the propensity back then, as now, to locate army bases as far back in the boon docks as possible, not any where close to a town where there was anything to do. They did a good job with us.

We were among the first troops there. We lived in tents and black mud.

We were paid $21.00 per month and netted $18.00 after deducts. That was pretty good when the best steak dinner was six bits, smokes fifteen cents a pack, gasoline fifteen cents a gallon, and so forth. The food sent down to us was good until the army cooks got through with it, but we ate it, and most gained weight.

We were trained how to start out with our left foot which is very important in civilian life. I have used it many times, also how to stay in line. This comes in handy even today especially in buffet lines. We learned how to walk long distances in the hot sun with very little water, and above all if you had any inhibitions when you came in, you soon lost them after sleeping side to side, bathing, and performing bodily functions with a bunch of men. Above all, you learned to instantly obey orders from someone who had half the education you had, and maybe half the brains.

One event that I vividly remember is when we were required to take an IQ test. Now I remember the officers telling us how important this test was. I don't remember them telling us that it would follow us all the rest of our career. Some of the boy's just half tried and laughed it off. It cost them in years to come.

If you remember the movie, "Patton" when he told the troops they wouldn't have to tell their kids that they spent the War shoveling manure in Louisiana. I didn't spend the War there but I spent three miserable weeks there sleeping in tents, no bath rooms, marching through mud, swatting mosquitoes, stepping on snakes, and doing without water, all under the command of incompetent officers.

I have had many important dates burned into my mind, when I got married, the birth of my children, when Kennedy got killed, but one stands out above all the rest, December 7, 1941 when Pearl Harbor was bombed. If that old camp was still there, even after sixty- four years, I could still find the spot where I heard the news.

Within a few weeks we were on a troop train headed for war and the young who had joined the army as boys were expected to become men and fight a war. More about life during the war at a later date.

THE REAL THING

As I mentioned before, Pearl Harbor changed everything. A bunch of country boys suddenly went from playing war to going to war. We country boys soon found ourselves on a Troop Train headed north.

All country boys, from one locality, who after the draft found themselves mixed up with people from all over the Country, every nationality, and every religion. There was culling process done, but it took awhile. We had one boy who had epileptic seizures, some who inflicted harm on themselves, homosexuals, now called gays, who rightly or wrongly back then, were called queers. Some really abused them while those who considered it an affliction felt sorry for them. All these were eventually weeded out of the service. We were on that slow moving train for seven days before reaching Ft. Lewis, Washington. The reason it took so long was, we had to give way to every other train on the track. Washington was quite a change. It was wet, cold, and we thought dreary. I spent my first Xmas eve away from home on guard duty out in the boon docks. As I gazed up at the bright stars I asked myself what I was doing there. That was the first and last time that I came close to feeling sorry for myself while in the service.

We had never seen many high hills in East Texas, much less mountains. We were in a barber shop one day and we looked out and saw Mt. Rainier off in the distance and we decided we might hike over there Saturday and climb it. We learned how green we really were when the barbers told us it was eighty miles away.

We spent time guarding railroad bridges, and the likes. Guarding against what I never found out. I do remember the rail cars coming by sometimes with just one big log on the car.

We were stationed in little towns like Kelso and Longview, WA. Probably more that I can't remember. It is a strange thing that as you get old you can remember some of the most minute and trivial things and yet cannot remember things that might have been important.

We moved out of Washington and down into Oregon. I do remember Portland Oregon by the way we were received by those rough long shore men who made their living loading and unloading the ships.

When you went into a bar or restaurant or any place they would not let you pay for anything. We always thought it was because of the way we talked. They had never heard the Kings English spoken the way we did. They took us into their homes, took us fishing, and many other kind things.

Another thing that reminds me of Portland is because of a girl I met. She was the first girl that I met after the war broke out. She was a very nice girl from a nice family that sort of took me in. When we moved I severed all ties to Portland like I had learned to do all my life with my family's frequent moves. You can't help but wonder what kind of life she and others have lived since the war.

On to Santa Rosa, California where several incidents stand out. We saw the filming of the movie "Shadow Of A Doubt" with Joseph Cotton and Teresa Wright. Another vivid incident was when I went to sleep and dropped a lighted cigarette on my bed and it burned a six inch hole through the four inch comforter, the sheet, my under shirt, and the mattress. I didn't have a mark on me. I have mentioned before about eating bear meat, cherries off the tree and so forth.

In California we guarded the coast line although with the weapons, and the training we had we could not have whipped a troop of Japanese girl scouts. My job was to patrol Highway 101, with mountains on one side and the ocean far below on the other side, at night in a jeep with no lights on.

My unit ended up in laid back San Francisco at a place called Fr. Chronkite, which was at the south end of the Golden Gate Bridge. It was there that I decided that I would try to better myself and apply for Officers Training School. That was the beginning of a completely new life for me.

LOOKING FOR HELP

At this advance stage of my life, I have come to the conclusion that I have been using the wrong kind of medical and dental care. I am looking for a dentist who wears false teeth. Preferably all his assistants also. There is no way that an office of people with a mouth full of pearly white teeth who can chew beef jerky without water and probably crack hickory nuts can have any idea what false teeth feel like, regardless of the schooling and books they have read. I can only imagine what President George Washington had to go through with his wooden teeth. It ain't much fun.

While we are looking, I need a doctor who suffers from flat feet, had occasional bouts of constipation and diarrhea, heartburn, sinus, infrequent pains from unknown source, uses salt on everything, and likes a couple shots of good whiskey in the evening to lubricate his conversation.

Don't give me one of those young ones who is gung ho with running shoes and those short pants with the alligator on them, who runs in marathons, and all that stuff. Who works out at the fitness center twice a week. I need one who has lived a life of dissipation like I have.

As to glasses. I would like to be fitted by someone who wears triple bifocals, who has a sore nose and ear from the frames, and who is constantly pushing the glasses back with his thumb. I would prefer one who couldn't read the first two lines of the chart with his glasses off or read a stop sign from ten feet. Also one who can't read the funny papers without a magnifying glass.

I am presently trying hearing aides for the third time. I keep expecting miracles, but really know better. This is another case of trying to find a provider that can put themselves in your shoes one who can interpret the whistles, hums and other sounds that emanate from them from time to time throughout the day and night. I think the only way is for them to wear hearing aides, the expensive kind. That doesn't apply to the gorgeous creature who is now working with me. Heaven forbid that. Maybe some older person to stand by for advice who can tell you that it will take a long time for your wife and friends to stop hollering at you. Also the new sound that you hear is not an approaching storm but the traffic in front of the house.

I have told Peggy to throw these contraptions away when I pass on but on second thought if I miss the cut and end up in the other place I will probably need them. That would be the ultimate punishment to have to wear these contraptions through out eternity. That should be enough to scare a person into trying harder to live a good life with what time he has left.

A New Life

Probably by now, with the exception of my grandchildren, you all have learned more about my WWII service than you wanted to, but I set out to recount it. It ends with this article.

When I left you I was on my way to Ft. Benning GA. For Officers Training School. It was designed to make an officer of us in ninety days. Nothing was mentioned about becoming a gentlemen as was the case in the movie.

The time was spent in hard physical training and basic education in the duties of an officer. We graduates were referred to as shave tails, or ninety day wonders. The darlings of the officer's class were the West Point graduates, which I guess was deserved because they spent four hard years earning their officer's bars.

We entered a whole new world where we were saluted instead of saluting, with our own quarters, dinning facilities, special officers club, and many more privileges. I was still a green country boy who was suddenly elevated way above his raising.

As soon as I finished the Infantry school, I was assigned to the Intelligence School. Why it was called this I don't know, because you didn't have to be that smart to get in as evidenced by my acceptance to the thing.

I was trained to be a Communications Officer, and since radios were not in use back then, we had to learn how to climb a telephone pole with those spike things on your legs. Learning the Morse Code, stringing telephone lines, and other things that I never had to do later because I had people who did all that.

When I completed this course, I was assigned to the 13th Airborne Division, stationed at Southern Pines, North Carolina. Where I became a Communication Officer in the 326th Glider Infantry. We were trained to fly in one of those cloth like kites with wings, which was a perfect target to shoot at on the way down, and usually wrecked itself when it landed.

Later on I completed Jump School where against all laws of nature, men jumped from high places, trusting in a piece of cloth to open and ease them to the ground. Looking back it's hard for me to believe that I did all this because I never was completely at ease in an airplane. Being like the old farmer who was talked into taking his first plane ride and when asked if he was scared said, "not really but I never did put all my weight down on it.

While there we did routine training while waiting to go into combat. I was in a couple of serious wrecks that marked my face up some. Also I was in special unit sent to Ft. Polk, La. Where we experimented in a glider pick up exercise where by a plane with a hook on it, snared a rope on the glider and jerked, and I mean jerked us into the air. One thing stands out in my memory was when I was in the hospital on Xmas eve in 1944, a group of carolers came by my room and left me a gift. I have never received a more appreciated gift.

We were finally sent to Europe to relieve the troops trapped at Bastogne. We spent seven days crowded on a troop ship with the men sleeping on hammocks in the hole of the ship, foul air, sea sick, and with the plumbing stopped up. It was just about as bad as the slave ships that we have read about except there was no one with whips.

We landed at La Harve, France where we boarded cattle cars for Sens, France. We arrived at night where I was directed to the house that I was to stay in. Because of the black out and the fact that I did not know a word of French I thought I would never find it. It was my luck to be assigned a house with a German collaborator living there who not only had her hair cut off but had a swastika painted on the guard wall. I soon moved to the hotel.

The stay there was real pleasant with the exception that my job was to censor my boys letters sent back home. It was to keep the Germans from learning where we were. They knew where we were before we got off the ship. It was another of the many stupid things the brass caused us to have to do.

Since Bastogne was secure we were scheduled to jump across the Rhine River and take the Remengen Bridge. Patton beat us to it and so we were loaded on ships on our way to Japan, which surrendered after the bombs were dropped. I have always thought that President Truman saved my life by having the guts to drop the bombs. If a situation like that arose today, and Congress had to make the decision, the bombs would never have been used regardless of the lives it might have saved.

When we reached the States I went to El Paso, Texas to have my face reworked, went to Mexico with my uncle, saw the bull fights, had lunch in a small Mexican town with a U.S. soldier who was in the last stages of alcoholism, spent a final three day fling in the Adolphus Hotel in Dallas, and on to Crockett.

In my advanced age I am a firm believer in fate. It had to be fate that guided me from a small East Texas town, all across the U.S. Into foreign countries, kept me out of harms way, and let me end up less that a hundred miles from where I was born, to meet the person that I wanted to spend the rest of my life with.

THE RAIN CROW

The other day when I was out in my garden I heard a rain crow calling. It took me back to my childhood when we believed that it was calling for rain and that it would rain three days later.

It was and is an elusive bird that I don't ever remember seeing. That was bourn out the other day when I couldn't locate him in a tree right over my head. That sucker must have been calling for rain all through June and July to bring on the rains that we have had.

Another elusive bird that was common in my childhood was the "Whip-poor-will." I remember in the stifling heat of a summer night when you had sweated your clothes and the sheets wet and desperate to get some sleep, hearing this bird call. That's another creature that I don't ever remember seeing.

Now I know that these birds and the many more creatures that were common then and now had scientific names which we knew nothing about but we knew them when we saw or heard them, and that's all that mattered

The Spreading Adder snake was an example. When it was disturbed it spread its hood like a cobra and when really disturbed, would open its mouth wide and play dead. It was really a puff adder and harmless.

Then there was the Devil's horse, a praying mantis, that we used to torment. Salamanders and pocket gophers a good cat could keep in check. Rattle snake pilots, copperheads that we killed on sight. Red headed woodpeckers and sap suckers that were fair game for our sling shots.

On a hot summer day when the Katy dids [actually locust] filled the air with its incessant noise and when the guineas chipped in, created a symphony of sound that only a lonely farm wife could appreciate.

Then on hot summer evenings the Bull bats, along with the little common bats, would circle under the street lights to catch bugs. We considered it great sport to knock the little buggers out of the air with fishing poles. You must remember back then there wasn't much to do between dark and bed time.

Another creature that we have today that many have never seen is the flying squirrel. It is a nocturnal animal that make the noise on your roof during the night. There used to be a big old rotten tree that housed a colony of them and when we pounded on it they would bail out and glide a long way to another tree, beautiful little things .

Back then in our care free days in the woods we knew about all of God's creatures. But today there are many that weren't there back then. Back then there were no Jack rabbits, no rattle snakes, no armadillos, no fire ants, no coyotes, no grackles, and no little Inca doves that make the beautiful calls.

Come to think of it there in our small isolated Northeast Texas town back then there were no Catholics, no Republicans, and no illegal Aliens either. I don't know how we made it but we did.

I stuck my head out a few minutes ago and heard that rain crow again. Since its going to rain in three days I am going to go out and plant a row of purple hull peas. Now that's one of God's gifts that will never change and we can give thanks for that.

Change Ready Or Not
- Like It Or Not

It is hard to realize what dramatic changes that we have under gone in just a few years. It was brought home to me when I picked up an issue of the Courier celebrating Houston County's one hundred fiftieth birthday.

I counted over forty business firms that are no more and I bet I missed a bunch. The Royal Café, W.B. Roberts Pest Control, Berry Gin Co, Buddies Grocery, Polk's, Hamns, Roger Shoe Store, Raymond's Men's Store, Casa Martinez, King's Inn , Shop-a-Lot, LaRue's Pharmacy, Six Beauty Shops, Car Dealership's, Tractor Company's, Lewis Smith Wrecking Yard, N.L. Asher's Shoe Store, Keeland, Overstreet Hardware, just to name a few.

The grocery prices back then. When I first saw them I was tempted to send Peggy to the grocery store to pick up some more stuff that we didn't need, until I noticed the 1987 date on the paper.

Eight oz. can biscuits –8cents, fresh pineapple 29 cents, hamburger 43 cents a pound, coffee 49 cents lb, 33 cents bottle for catsup, cracker barrel cheese 66 cents lb. and so forth. Cars, five to seven thousand dollars, and a pickup for less. Gasoline was only thirty cents per gallon.

All these changes were not our doing. They were the result of economics that came with the times. Most have been for the better. Our standard of living today is far superior to those back then. Our income today would have been unheard of even for the people back then that we considered affluent.

The changes that are hard for my generation to accept are the fault of my generation. We sold out to the Federal Government for money and with that transaction we lost our local right to govern and even threw in our common sense to boot.

We let the Federal Government cram programs, though well intended, down our throats that had the opposite effect from that intended. Everybody knew that segregation was wrong and needed to be changed, but the way it was done may have changed the physical aspect of mixing the races, but the hoped for healing that should have resulted has not completely come about.

Another stupid Government program is the "Endangered Species Act." Not so much the law itself but the fact that it was turned over to idiots to enforce.

I am certainly in favor of protecting some creature that is of value to most of the people. But to hold up worth while projects costing the tax payer untold millions just because it might disturb the sex life of a tinny minnow that few had ever seen is ridiculous. Alligators, wolves, snakes, every kind of bird, you name it is on the list. The main endangered species is the American Taxpayer. He is disappearing faster than some of the critters that are listed.

You have heard a great deal about the so called "N" word lately. It denotes a word that is used freely between those of certain races, but is considered racist. Perhaps rightly so, for other races to use the word.

Now we are confronted with the "M" word. This describes a race of people from across the Rio Grande that are, if left unchecked, are in the process of taking over our country. You are going to see every one of the twelve million already here become citizens. Because they are demanding it from a government that doesn't know what to do about the problem. Maybe they can do a better job than some of us.

Now there is another race that deserves to be mentioned and to continue this initial only farce we shall refer to as the "W" race. This is the people who founded a great nation founded on the principles of hard work, honest, sanctity of marriage, faith in God, freedom of expression, and justice for all. This is the race that pays most of the bills for the other two.

We have all been taught that one person can change a lot of things and we have found that to be true. I have thought a lot about that lately. Like the other day when an "M" person was cleaning the house and when some "M" people were blowing the leaves off the yard, and I was waiting for another "M" person to work my garden, I thought we ought to send all the "M" people back across the border, well some anyway. The ones who work for me won't make that much difference so maybe they should stay.

I have read a great deal about one person making a difference. I thought why don't I try to do something that can make a difference. All I have to do is to make a start. Now let's see, Saturday is football all day, Sunday is church and football, Monday night I play poker and I have to think about that, Tuesday I have a dentist appointment, Wednesday a Church function to go to, Thursday a doctors appointment, Friday and "M" person is coming to work my garden, and Saturday is foot ball again.

Just as soon as I can work it into my schedule I am going to think about making some changes.

AN ADDRESS TO THE CROCKETT ROTARY CLUB

The club was chartered in 1937 with Dr. Paul Stokes its first president. It initially met in the Royal Café, then in Carl Murray's home, and then to the Crockett Hotel. A list of the charter members reads like a who's, who of Crockett's influential citizens

They were responsible for some of the early improvements such as the 35 acre Davy Crockett Park and its original buildings. The majestic pecan trees that you see all over town just didn't spring up nor were they planted by Indians. They were planted during the 1936 Texas Centennial as a community project with the Boy Scouts planting many of them. For a long time Crockett was known as the city of 5000 people and 10,000 pecan trees.

Some twenty years later when I joined the club many of these old time members were becoming less active. I do remember in December of 1955 the club planted the pine tree on the NE corner of the courthouse lawn as a Xmas tree. At that stage of the game many old members came just for the fellowship and good food. One committee that they always maintained was the "Railroad Committee" with Herbert Callaway as chairman. When asked for the railroad report he solemnly reported that the trains were running.

The old ones got a kick out of that.

When WWII was declared Crockett and Houston County had not really moved into the 19th century. Cotton was king and the whole economy revolved around it. Crockett alone had five gins and on Saturday, Camp St. and surrounding streets were jammed full of wagons and teams and it was hard to walk West of Goliad.

Many of Crockett's young men and women went into the Service and saw places that they never dreamed of. When they finally came home they had seen the "elephant" and wanted change.

With the formation of the Jaycees things began to change. With the support of this club, the Lions Club, and the older leaders, the pace picked up and results began to show.

Crockett is 150 miles form 70% of the population of Texas and 200 miles from 90%. Five major highways pass through the town before the Loop, it all had to cross the square. To make it worse, Lee's China Inn extends 12 feet into city Right of Way, making that a bottleneck. Back then when you told some one you were from Crockett "Oh yeah, the dangerous square and the best chicken fried steaks in Texas."

In 1955 some Crockett leaders went to Austin and asked for a by pass around the town. We were the first town in Texas to ask for a loop and the smallest town in Texas with a loop completely around it. Also at a later date a paved road to the Country Club and the Northcutt woodworking plant was secretly brought about.

To progress, Houston County needed an airport. The leaders furnished the money from their own pockets to buy the land and gave it to the County. The County like Leroy didn't want the ball but public pressure prevailed. They took it making improvements down through the years. It still does not have a needed fence around it to keep livestock, wild animals, and irate housewives off the runway.

The water you drink today comes from a 1,500 acre lake producing seven and one half million gallons of pure water daily. This lake didn't come easy either. It took work and lots of work.

With electricity, water, and telephones you can live anywhere in the County with City conveniences. This has caused an unexpected phenomenal event. That is the rapid exodus of people from the towns to the country. When they leave they take their talents with them creating a vacuum in our city and county governments. The vacuum is being filled by mostly unqualified people to the extent that it has almost become joke, albeit it is a serious one.

If I were a business or professional person who depended on Crockett for the future welfare of my family I would be concerned, gravely concerned. I would want to see some changes made now before it is too late. Time is running out.

There is enough talent in this room to make a start. It sometimes just takes one person to ignite a spark. Each of you should ask yourself this question, "If not I, who? If not now, when?"

Whoever that person may be I wish them well.

THE FAMILY REUNION

Last week we hosted the yearly Mattox Family Reunion. Now August isn't the best time to have such an event but a nephew scheduled it around his vacation and his convenience. It is always held here at the old Knox cabin at the County Club Lake.

Every year we are told that we are getting too old to host the event and that they will bring everything. Sounds good.? On Saturday, Peggy told me to go to the grocery store and get some snacks for them to have when the first shift arrived Sunday afternoon. Also to get a bunch of different kinds of cold drinks. I asked "What are THEY bringing? She said that they would need coffee, orange juice, and some kind of breakfast rolls for Monday morning. Again "What are THEY bringing?"

They will come to the house Sunday night and they want a vegetable supper from the garden that you have been bragging about. Go to the store and get about two dozen pork chops, potatoes, and bananas for the pudding. We are going to have fried pork chops, gravy, purple hull peas, mashed potatoes, collard greens, boiled okra, cornbread, and slang jang. Now this last concoction needs some explaining. First I don't know where it or the name originated. My Mother and grandmother made it and they didn't know.

It consists of equal part of onions, bell peppers, cucumbers, and tomatoes. The marinade is 1/3 cup of vinegar (I prefer 5% white), 2/3 cup water, salt, pepper, and sugar. I add some cilantro t mine. Now my mother and grandmother didn't use cilantro because they had never heard of it. I have only learned of it since the Mexicans took back Texas. My kids and grandkids love it. We fed ten people Sunday night and they cleaned up everything in spite of some of them claiming to be on a diet.

I was told to go get a bunch of cereal for Monday's breakfast, because that's what they ate. Again "What are **THEY** bringing?" Monday night's menu was almost the same with roast beef, gravy, zipper cream peas, cream potatoes, okra gumbo, cornbread, slang jang, and cake. We fed twenty people at the cabin. None claiming to being on a diet.

Tuesday morning I was informed that my older sister would love some quail for breakfast like the old days. Peggy knew that I had some quail in the freezer so quail it was. Quail, hot biscuits, gravy, grits, jelly, and the last of the orange juice. We just fed eight that morning. The first shift left Sunday night, the second shift Tuesday afternoon, and the last shift, Wednesday. Our house looked liked the locust had hit it. Most of my pickles, all my cucumbers, tomatoes, peppers, okra and squash from the garden, gone from this house.

Since then we have gotten many e-mails, no letters, telling us what a great time they had and saying they can hardly wait till next year. We always reply how glad we were to have them and hope we will be alive next year. We don't tell them that it will probably take us a year to get over this one.

After they had all gone and things had gotten some what back to normal, I again asked Peggy, "Did <u>THEY</u> bring anything?" She said if <u>THEY</u> did, she didn't notice it.

A Near Experience

The recent writings about Mother Teresa's bout with her faith brought home a memory of an event that happened long ago. I have never discussed this in detail with anyone but Peggy. Since it is part of my WWII experiences that my children and grandchildren want to learn about I will relate it.

In December of 1944 just before Christmas a friend and I were on our way from Southern Pines, N.C. to Dillion, S. C. to a party. It was a rainy night and as we approached a hill, another car topped the hill on our side of the road.

My friends car had no horn, so as a former race car driver his impulse was to turn sharply to the left. The other driver, who would later prove to be drunk, turned to the right causing a head on collision. My face went through the windshield, no seat belts or shatter proof glass back then, causing serious cuts on my face and breaking a finger.

My first conscious reaction was to try to rouse my friend. I learned later that he was killed instantly. I heard someone crying for help so I got out of the car and was bleeding so bad from cuts across my eye brows that I had to walk bent over to the other car. His legs were penned in the car and his shoulder was on the pavement. He asked me to help him. I won't tell you what I told him.

My next memory was riding in the back of a car with a man holding my head. It must have been and older model because I could hear the blood dripping on the floor. This man was urging his companion to drive faster because he said I was bleeding to death.

Now if you think this won't grab you. I thought here, I am a twenty four year old man, been in the Army four years. Never fired a shot for my Country, never really made a contribution to society, about to die on a lonely road in South Carolina, of all places.

My next conscious memory was drifting in and out from the "Land Of Sweet Forever," then jolted back by a terrible thirst. All this time a soft hand held mine and soothing words were whispered in my ear. I though at the time that it was an Angel and am still not sure that it wasn't.

This was Friday night and I came to Monday morning on the operating table as I heard the Army doctors discussing what a mess I was in with my face swollen and full of shattered glass. There were many excuses why it took three days to get me sewed up. I knew they probably couldn't find any sober Army doctors to do it any sooner. For the job done on me I am not sure they were sober that Monday morning. I had to later get plastic surgery done on my face to get out some more glass and remove some scars.

Then we move to Christmas Eve at my base hospital and I was the only patient on my ward. I still could not see being wrapped in bandages, but I could hear the beautiful strains of "Silent Night" down the hall. I thought, please let them come in here which they did. Right then I was reunited with my angel when the same soft hand and beautiful voice wished me a Merry Christmas and a speedy recovery. It was pretty hard not to feel sorry for myself that night.

They didn't have to tell me later that my experience in the Dillion hospital was with a Catholic nun, and my base hospital experience was with a beautiful church volunteer. Well, deep down I knew that, but I would still like to think that they could be wrong. I know that I experienced something that will stay with me forever.

OLD TIMES DERE BUT NOT FORGOTTEN

It's been years since I have paid the bills around this house and quite a while since I even paid attention to the heading on the things. So when I happened to pick up the mail from the floor the other day I noticed some of them.

Now Northland Cable certainly I recognized, because we have had it a long time. Dish Network made me think, until I figured it was for the satellite system that was given to us years ago by a niece who wanted us to be sure and watch her kids play golf.

Centerpoint , now that threw me. What made them change the name of United Gas & Entex to Centerpoint? What could be more centered and to the point than the United Gas Co., run by old reliable crew of Dale Leediker, John Shaver, David Sepmoree, and others whom we relied on to take care of us and are sorely missed.

Then came Reliant energy. When I inquired, I was told that it was our electricity supplier and that I had just signed a new contract that saved us three cents a kilowatt hour. What is a kilowatt hour for God sakes, and what happen to Texas Power & Light Co?

Old reliable TP&L back when they were the leader in community affairs and where every inquiry was greeted by a cheerful voice. Where every problem big or small got attention of either Mr. Claude Brown, who was the manager when I first came here, or later Wilse Hail, George McKinney and Tom Milford. All gentlemen of the old school.

If the problem was outside, Hershel Boles, Ben Erwin, and others would take care of it. If it was inside, Dewitt Rains, with his cheerful attitude, would be at your door almost before you hung up the phone. This is unheard of today.

Windstream took some explaining. It's our telephone company. Telephones take me way back to the time I first set foot in Crockett over sixty years ago. The founder of the Crockett Telephone Co. was Mr. John Cook, Louis Cooks, grandfather, was still living, but the company was run by Loch Cook, Louis Cooks father.

The ones who really kept it going was chief operator, Mrs. Beaty and operators, Edith Pitts, later Conaway, the Hallmark sisters, and others working on the inside and Garland Ellis and later Clem Copus on the outside.

Later the company was sold to J.B. McDuff with the promise of a County wide dial telephone system that was supposed to speed up the service. We really didn't appreciate how fast our old service was. Back then you could pick up the phone, don't worry about a number, just tell one of the girls who you wanted. If the person was at home they would connect you, if not they would tell you where the person had gone.

It really came in handy if you wanted a doctor. They would run him down for you. It was really better than CNN news in finding out what was going on in Crockett, because it had a personal touch that is unknown today.

Now I mentioned that Loch Cook ran the company. Now Mr. Cook could decide if you got a telephone, but Garland Ellis and later Clem Copus decided when you got it. They enjoyed an independence of action that would be unheard of today. If you needed a telephone in a hurry it was wise to cultivate their friendship.

Now I know young people get tired of hearing old people talking about the past. But you must remember that most of our life has passed and since that is where the memories lie that's where we live

I want to share these cherished memories with you because that kind of life is truly gone with the wind and has settled into the dust we walk on.

ONE MAN'S OPINION

In this day of political correctness and social concerns it is rare to find someone who will express an opinion, especially in public. Andy Rooney, the old curmudgeon on the CBS. sixty minute program did, and I quote, " I don't think being a minority makes you a victim of anything except numbers. The only things that I can think of that are truly discriminatory are thing like United Negro College Fund, Jet Magazine, Black Entertainment Television, and Miss Black America. Try to have thing like the United Caucasian College Fund, Cloud magazine, White Entertainment Television, or Miss White America, and see what happens...Jessie will be knocking down your door.

Guns do not make you a killer. I think killing makes you a kill. You can kill someone with a baseball bat or a car, but no one is trying to ban you from driving to the ball game. I believe they are called Boy Scouts for a reason, that is why there are no girls allowed. Girls belong in the Girl Scouts. ARE YOU LISTENING MARTHA BURKE?

I thing that if you feel homosexuality is wrong, it is not a phobia, it is an opinion. I have the right NOT to be tolerant of others because they are different, weird, or tick me off. When 70% of the people who get arrested are black, in cities where70% of the population is black that is not racial profiling, it is the law of Probability.

I believe that if you are selling me a milkshake, a pack of cigarettes, a newspaper, or a hotel room, you must do it in English! As a matter of fact. If you want to be an American citizen, you should have to speak English. My father and grandfather didn't die in vain so you can leave the countries you were born in to come over and disrespect ours.

I think the police should have every right to shoot you if you threaten them after they tell you to stop. If you can not understand the word "freeze" or "stop" in English, see the above lines. I don't think just because you were not born in this country, you are qualified for any special loan programs, government sponsored bank loans, or tax breaks, ect. So you can open a hotel, coffee shop, trinket store, or any other business.

We did not go to the aid of certain foreign countries and risk our lives in wars to defend their freedoms, so that decades later they could come over here and tell us our constitution is a living document, and open to their interpretations. I don't hate the rich. I don't pity the poor. I know pro wrestling is fake, but so are movies, and television. That doesn't stop you from watching them. I think that Bill Gates has every right to keep every penny he has made and continues to make more. If it ticks you off go and invent the next operating system that's better and put your name on the building.

It doesn't take a whole village to raise a child right, but it does take a parent to stand up to the kid, and smack their little behinds when necessary, and say 'No!" I think tattoos and piercing are fine if you want them but please don't pretend they are a political statement. And please stay home until that new lip ring heals. I don't want to look at your ugly infected mouth as you serve me French fries.

I am sick of "Political Correctness." I know a lot of black people and not a single one of them was born Africa, so how can they be "African –Americans?" Beside Africa is a continent. I don't go around saying I am European-American because my great, great, great, great, great grandfather was from Europe. I am proud to be from America and nowhere else. And if you don't like my view, tough…"

As the words of a popular hip song say: "What say you? What say you?

College Mascots

I noticed in the paper the other day that Texas A&M was looking for a new mascot to replace the aging Reveille. Mascots are an important part of a college athletic program with little impact on the academic side. Some are actual animals, birds, or other species , while others are only symbols.

Now Texas has Bevo, the huge neutered long horn whose sole activity during an athletic contest is to lie there, chewing his cud, and occasionally pooping on the grass. Between the contest, he enjoys the same routine.

Texas Tech Red Raiders have a black horse, you wonder why no red one, tearing around the field topped off with a terrified rider also in black, desperately trying to stay on. This mascot probably spends some bored time between games.

Same with Oklahoma with its Sooner Wagon, SMU with Purina, Baylor with its bear, and so forth. Many people think that the TCU mascot is only a symbol but legend says they actually have a horned frog on a leash at the games parading up and down the side lines too small to be seen with the naked eye.

All this is to say that most mascots serve no useful purpose between athletic contests. Not so with Texas A&M, they have a dog mascot who between games can chase rabbits, tree squirrels, coons and possums, to provide food for the Corp. Now that's a useful mascot that earns its keep.

That remind me of a mascot story while a freshman at A&M. We had lost our mascot and were using a little cocker spaniel that belonged to senior named Mattox from El Paso. How I got acquainted with him I can't remember. Since I worked on week ends many times, he asked me to keep little Freckles. It happened so often that Freckles and I became good friends to the point that she would not stay with her owner. One time she even found me in a crowded movie theater, after that he kept her tied up.

My grand kids would not believe that I once ate and slept with a college mascot. As Red Buttons used to say; "strange things happen."

Old Customs

As I grow older I have more people, especially young ones, asking me about people and events that happened long ago in Crockett and Houston County. I am not a native of Crockett having come here in 1946 after WWII. But when I think about all those who have gone before me and the condition of some of those who are left I realize that the inquirers are left without much choice.

I realize how difficult it must be for the younger generation to really believe the tales about some of the conditions and customs that used to exist. To hear that even after the War there would be so many wagons and teams around Camp Street and that area on Saturday that you could hardly find an empty space. That West Goliad would be jammed with people and both movie theaters would be full. The custom was to come to town on Saturday to visit and shop all day. Many wore shoes that they were not used wearing which originated the saying, "I going to the wagon yard, these shoes are killing me."

Before my time where Barkley Funeral home is now and Sullivan Motor used to be there was once a livery stable, where if you stayed a day or two, you could board your horses or mules. On the west side of the present Knox Furniture Store the old elevator is still in use that used to take the wagons up to the second floor to be stored. The old Pickwick Hotel, the Schmitt House, and maybe others offered a place to stay.

Another thing that has passed was "sitting up with the dead." This originated in pioneer times when someone died. The neighbors would come, bring food, help prepare the body for burial, usually the next day, and sit for the night. This served two purposes, one to comfort the family, and in many cases where the house was poorly constructed to keep unwanted animals out.

This custom existed here Houston County well up into the nineteen sixties and maybe the seventies. If you happened to know someone, even causally, and one of their relatives how ever distant died, you would be called upon by the funeral home to sit up with the body. I doubt if the friend even knew who sat up with Aunt Lucy or Uncle Tom. I have been called to do this many times. You sat in shifts, if I remember, maybe three men, never women. The first shift from ten to twelve, the second twelve to two. And third, two to four. I don't remember anyone after four AM. Being young and naïve I always got the two to four shifts.

I have had many experiences in my sitting up, some amusing. One night three of us were sitting up with someone that I didn't know. When a friend of ours rushed in apologizing for being late. After a while someone mentioned who we were sitting with. The new arrival realized that he should be at the other funeral home and he took off in a hurry.

One of the hardest things was to have to sit up when the body was brought home. One such night that I was sitting, about every hour the distraught widow would come in and throw herself on the coffin crying and carrying on.

That night was memorable for the above, but also when my shift ended at two AM my relief came in. Now this man was known for his loud voice when sober but he came in drunk, and even his whisper would arouse the dead. The girls staying with the widow were scared and I had to stay until daylight.

I guess one event that you would expect to see only in a movie happened to Peggy and I one night when we sere sitting the two to four shift. Some house guest came in late and opened the coffin to take some pictures. After everything quieted down suddenly we heard a terrible squalling noise coming from the living room where the body was. When I got in there the woman's pet cat was sitting on her chest making the terrible noise we heard. I guess the cat got in when the guest came in. I was pretty shaken up and so was the cat when I threw it out.

Some customs we old ones wish might come back but, not sitting up with the dead. Modern funeral homes not only keep cats and things our, but you do not have to dread getting the two to four shift.

Getting with It

For years my children and grandchildren have been telling me that I need to "get with it." I thought I was with it. I live in a house that can go from summer to winter at the push of a button. Several telephones, as opposed to none as when I was growing up during the depression.

Television sets, in color no less, that are a long way from our first radio. That set was about the size of a box of crackers, but could belt out the Light Crust Dough Boys, The Stamps Quartet, and The Bewely Mills Gang, at noon for all the neighbor to hear.

I have a dish and clothes washers and dryers. A contraption that filters the air. No iron clothes, men's ties that come down to the waist, automatic sprinkler system that waters the lawn and garden.

I have one of those "cell" phones that we get about three calls a year on, that I hold up to my ear with one hand and a bottle of water (city water that is) in the other, while I drive my pickup that has automatic transmission, power steering, air conditioning, and a tape player, around the square using only my elbows.

Then there is this fancy computer that refutes the old saying that "Father Know Best" by demonstrating that the younger a person is the smarter they get. I just thought that "I was with it."

I just found out what really "getting with it" entails when my daughter-in-law gave me a pair of Crocs. For those who don't have them let me explain. They are out of a molded piece of rubber made in China or Uganda, or somewhere else and probably cost less than two dollars to make.

They come in two lengths, too long, and too short. They are wide enough for Bigfoot to feel comfortable in. The have thirteen holes in the top to let rain water in and seven large holes in the soles to let the water out, and to provide easy access for fire ants. They have won every ugly contest that they have entered. Why is everyone buying them you ask? Because, by George they are comfortable. Men and women from all walks of life and professions are wearing them.

They are making their mark because for the first time in history women are wearing shoes that fit them and are comfortable and still feel like they "are with it."

WINDS OF FATE

Life's evenings sun is sinking low, the time draws near for me to go, to meet the deeds that I have done. Where the four winds blow, been there done that long ago, any regrets left to the mercy of the wind.

Memory failing for contemporary endeavors, but a kaleidoscope of vivid memories of the past flash by, some trivial, some momentous. With folded hands, now I lay me down to sleep, Jesus loves me. Early times, tent city road camp, sound of animals, cursing teamsters, soap in mouth for mimicking.

Dead cow, unborn calf, neighbors oyster feast, men eating them raw, first school, radio, Dempsey lost. On to new town, security of kinfolk, new school, new friends to seek. Barefoot, running free, pay check to pay check, never enough, rabid dogs, boils, sore eyes, itch, spankings, loving teacher, first pony, first love, first kiss.

Follow the job, good bye to friends, and first love. Not to look back. Depression, menial job, long hours, low pay no future. Lacking new friends, and new love. Army deemed salvation, started lowest, advanced some, start of a new life of over five year.

To Army life and as the winds of fate blow harder disregard the unknown future, eat, drink and be merry, throw away money, women to love, in love with none. Debt to U.S.

paid, home to a new town, finally true love, married, first born almost lost, second born lost.

Worked hard, to be safe and secure from all alarms, still striving. After many years of a long journey the circle is almost complete ending within a hundred miles of the beginning, back to the only home town I have ever known, where a burial spot awaits me.

After almost four score years, I think the journey through life is best expressed in a poem by William Randolph Hearst entitled:

"The Song of the River"

" The snow melts on the mountain and the water runs down to the spring, And the spring in a turbulent fountain with a song of youth to sing,
Runs down the riotous river, and the river flows to the sea,
And the water again goes back in the hill in rain where it used to be.

And I wonder if life's deep mystery isn't like the rain and the snow,
Returning through all eternity to the places it used to know,
For life was born on the lofty heights and flows in a laughing stream, then revisited,
To the river below whose onward flow ends in a peaceful dream.

And so at last, when our life has passed and river has run its course,
It again goes back, O'er the self same track to the mountains which was its source.

So why prize life or why fear death, or dread what used to be?
The river runs its allotted span till it reached the silent sea,
Then the water harked back to the mountain top to begin its course once more,
So we shall run the course begun till we reach the silent shore.

Then revisit earth in a pure rebirth from the heart of the virgin snow,
So don't ask why we live or die, or whither, or when we go,
Or wonder about the mysteries that only God can know."